First World War
and Army of Occupation
War Diary
France, Belgium and Germany

46 DIVISION
Divisional Troops
7 Belgium Artillery Regiment
1 August 1915 - 30 December 1916

WO95/2675/1

The Naval & Military Press Ltd
www.nmarchive.com
Published in association with The National Archives

Published by

The Naval & Military Press Ltd

Unit 10 Ridgewood Industrial Park,

Uckfield, East Sussex,

TN22 5QE England

Tel: +44 (0) 1825 749494

www.naval-military-press.com

www.nmarchive.com

This diary has been reprinted in facsimile from the original. Any imperfections are inevitably reproduced and the quality may fall short of modern type and cartographic standards.

Contents

Document type	Place/Title	Date From	Date To
Heading	WO95/2675/1 7 Belgium Artillery Regiment		
Heading	46th Division. Belgium Artillery Regt. Vol VI August 15		
Heading	War Diary for Aug. 1915 of Col. Dechesne's Group 7th Regt. Belgium Art les 1 Battn. B Bty 81st Bde R.F.A.		
War Diary		01/08/1915	31/08/1915
Miscellaneous	17 Div Arty For Information 3rd Division Appendix XXIII	03/08/1915	03/08/1915
Miscellaneous	Bde. R.Q. 3rd Divn. App XXIV	05/08/1915	05/08/1915
Operation(al) Order(s)	Operation Order No. 1 by Colonel Dechesne App XXIV	05/02/1915	05/02/1915
Miscellaneous	(SD) Dechgone. Col. Coy. Group.	05/08/1915	05/08/1915
Miscellaneous	A Form. Messages And Signals. App XXV		
Operation(al) Order(s)	8th Bde Operation Order No. 4 App XXVI	08/08/1915	08/08/1915
Miscellaneous	A Form. Messages And Signals. App. XXVII		
Miscellaneous	A Form. Messages And Signals.		
Miscellaneous	A Form. Messages And Signals. App XXVIII		
Miscellaneous	O.C. Dechesne's Group App XXIX	10/08/1915	10/08/1915
Miscellaneous	3rd Divisional Artillery Operation Order (on 3rd Division O.O. No. 26.) App XXX	18/08/1915	18/08/1915
Miscellaneous	Divisional Artillery Orders. by Brigadier General Herbert M. Campbell, Commanding 46th: Divisional Artillery App XXXI	19/08/1915	19/08/1915
Heading	The O C Re-Group		
Miscellaneous	O.C. Dechesne's Group App XXXII	20/08/1915	20/08/1915
Miscellaneous	The O C B/8 The Bde R F A	21/08/1915	21/08/1915
Operation(al) Order(s)	Operation Orders. No. 14 by Brigadier General C.T. Shipley. Commanding 139th Infantry Brigade. App XXXIII	21/08/1915	21/08/1915
Operation(al) Order(s)	46th. Divisional Artillery Operation Order No. 12 App XXXIV	21/08/1915	21/08/1915
Heading	46th Division. War Diary. 7th-Regiment Belgium Field Artillery September Vol VII		
War Diary		01/09/1915	30/09/1915
War Diary		25/09/1915	30/09/1915
War Diary		15/09/1915	15/09/1915
War Diary		06/09/1915	06/09/1915
War Diary		25/09/1915	30/09/1915
War Diary		01/09/1915	30/09/1915
War Diary		25/09/1915	30/09/1915
Heading	D A G 3rd Ech Base		
Heading	46th Division. October War Diary of 7th Belgium Regiment Field Artillery. Attached 24th Division. Vol VIII		
War Diary		01/10/1915	31/10/1915
War Diary		08/10/1915	08/10/1915
War Diary		06/10/1915	19/10/1915
War Diary		01/10/1915	31/10/1915
War Diary		01/11/1915	30/11/1915
War Diary		04/11/1915	16/11/1915

Miscellaneous	War Diary (Carbon Duplicate) of 7th Belgium Field Artillery.		
War Diary		01/12/1915	20/12/1915
War Diary		19/12/1915	31/12/1915
War Diary		02/12/1915	16/12/1915
War Diary		12/12/1915	27/12/1915
Heading	War Diary for February 1916. 7th-Regiment Belgium Field Artillery Vol XII		
War Diary		01/02/1916	29/02/1916
Heading	War Diary for March 1916 Of 7th-Belgium Field Artillery, attd & Corps (3rd & 50th Div) B.E.F. Vol XIII		
War Diary		01/03/1916	20/03/1916
Heading	War Diary of 7th Belgium Field Artillery. For April 1916 Vol XIV		
War Diary		01/04/1916	29/04/1916
Heading	War Diary of 7th-Belgium Field Artillery For May 1916 Vol 15		
War Diary		01/05/1916	13/05/1916
War Diary		01/05/1916	28/05/1916
Heading	War Diary for Month Of June 1916 Of 7th Belgium Field Artillery Attached Canadian Corps Vol 16		
War Diary		01/06/1916	09/06/1916
Heading	War Diary of 7th Belgium Field Artillery Attached Canadian Corps For July 1916 Vol 17		
War Diary		01/07/1916	31/07/1916
War Diary		14/07/1916	14/07/1916
War Diary		09/07/1916	30/07/1916
Miscellaneous	D.A.G. 3rd Echelon.	31/08/1916	31/08/1916
Heading	War Diary for August 1916 of 7th Belgium Field Artillery Vol 18		
War Diary		01/08/1916	31/08/1916
Miscellaneous	D.A.G. 3rd Echelon.	01/10/1916	01/10/1916
Heading	War Diary for September 1916 of 7th Belgium Field Artillery Vol 19		
War Diary		01/09/1916	20/09/1916
Miscellaneous	Casualties during month.	00/09/1916	00/09/1916
Miscellaneous	D.A.G. 3rd Echelon.	31/10/1916	31/10/1916
Heading	War Diary for October 1916 of 7th Belgium Field Artillery Vol 20		
War Diary		01/10/1916	31/10/1916
War Diary		12/10/1916	23/10/1916
Miscellaneous	D.A.G. 3rd Echelon.	30/11/1916	30/11/1916
Heading	War Diary of 7th Belgium Field Artillery For November 1916 Vol 21		
War Diary		01/11/1916	30/11/1916
Miscellaneous	Casualties during month.	01/11/1916	01/11/1916
Miscellaneous	D.A.G. 3rd Echelon.	31/12/1916	31/12/1916
Heading	War Diary for December 1916 of 13th (Old 7th) Belgium Field Artillery Vol 22		
War Diary		01/12/1916	30/12/1916

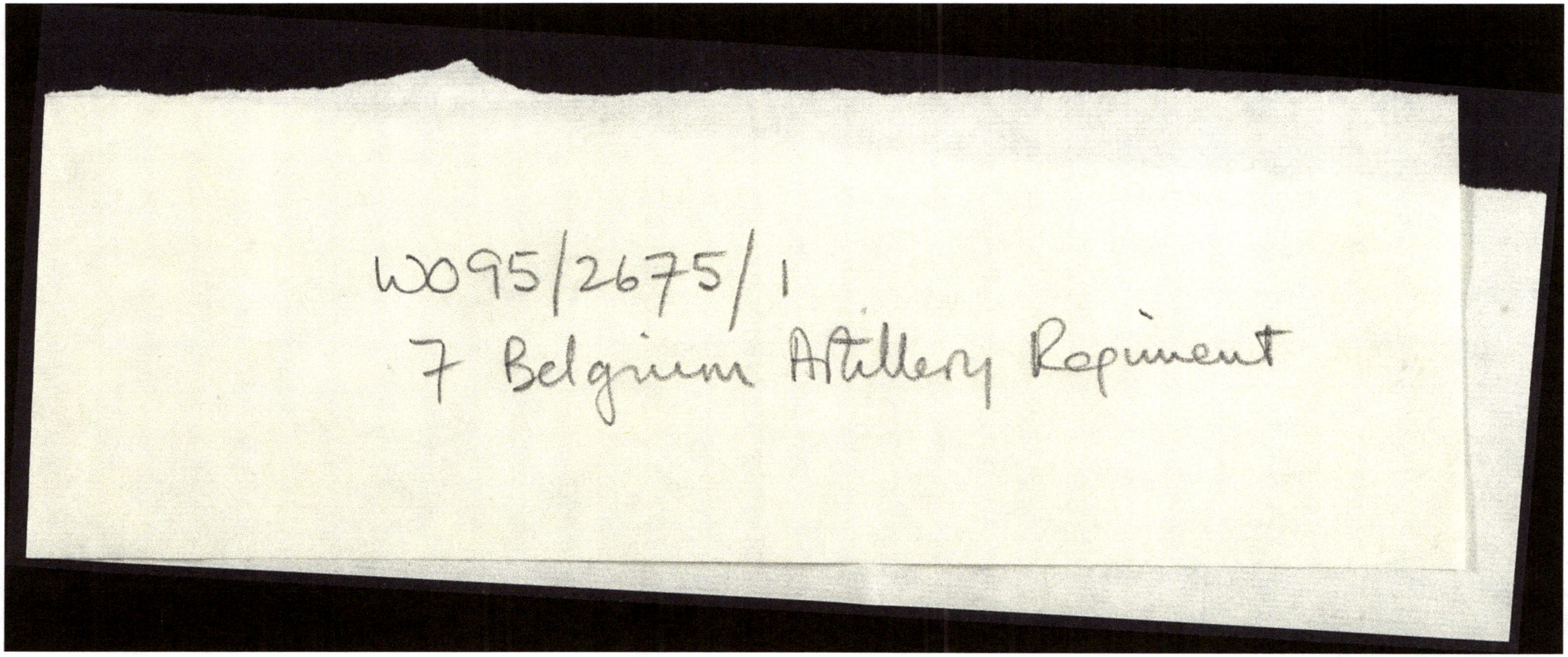

WO95/2675/1
7 Belgium Artillery Regiment

46th Division

121/6754

Belgium Artillery Regt.

Vol VI

August 15

Confidential

War Diary for Aug. 1915
of
Col. Dickson's Group.
7th Rgt. Belgian Art.
less 1 Battery
& 'B' Bty 51st Bde
R.F.A.

46th (N.M.) Divn.

Kept by
Captain C.L.D. Bridge
R.A.

Instructions regarding War Diaries and Intelligence Summaries are contained in F. S. Regs., Part II. and the Staff Manual respectively. Title Pages will be prepared in manuscript.

WAR DIARY
or
~~INTELLIGENCE SUMMARY~~
(Erase heading not required.)

Army Form C. 2118

(60)

Place	Date	Hour	Summary of Events and Information	Remarks and references to Appendices
	~~July~~ 1st Aug		During night all Btys of Left Group continued to shell occasionally the following pts. which will afterwards be referred to as "Roads etc in their Sector"	
			1st } 3rd } Road running immediately behind German Trenches in O4 & I34	
			4th Same road & road running round E side of 'hill 60' & ZWARTELEEN.	
			5th Road in O4 a91 Cross Road O4 C44 & HOLLEBEKE village	
			6th Same Road as 1st & 3rd Btys.	
			B/81 O12 b49 & O5 b86.	
		11. am	B/81 shelled N & S. Lodges of HOLLEBEKE CHATEAU (O4d) (12 Sh)	
		During Day	Btys again shelled as follows:-	
			1st & 3rd as above	
			4th at I35 a42 I29 a51 - 3.3 (Village) I29 c51 (Road crossing) I35 a (edge of wood) I29 c 62 (Hill 60)	
			5th Roads O4 - O10 & O11 - O12 - HOLLEBEKE & the road N & S of this village	
			6th Roads behind the Trenches. - (in all 127 Shrap.)	
		1 pm	Two 15 cm HE were fired by Germans 40x over posn of B/81	
		7.30 pm	Eight 15 cm HE - - - - onto posn of B/81	C.S.
	Aug. ~~July~~ 2nd	5 am	Twelve 15 cm HE were fired onto posn of B/81	
		9. am.	O.C. B/81 decided to move his Bty to a new posn at H24 7.4	
		11.7 am	4th Bty shelled 33 Register at request of O.C. R. Scots as Reprisals (8 HE) - one shell unfortunately fell in Trench 34, Killed one & wounded 4 men.	
		During Day	All Btys fired on frequented pts behind the German Trenches (126 Shrap.)	
		4.20 pm	3rd Bty shelled 28 Register (7 Shrap.)	
		5.6 pm 5.37 pm	1st Bty fired 36 HE at a German T.M opp. 31 - as Reprisal	C.B.

1875 Wt. W593/826 1,000,000 4/15 J.B.C. & A. A.D.S.S./Forms/C. 2118.

Instructions regarding War Diaries and Intelligence Summaries are contained in F. S. Regs., Part II. and the Staff Manual respectively. Title Pages will be prepared in manuscript.

WAR DIARY
or
~~INTELLIGENCE SUMMARY~~
(Erase heading not required.)

Army Form C. 2118

(61)

Place	Date	Hour	Summary of Events and Information	Remarks and references to Appendices
7	2/8/15	1 p.m.	2nd By. shelled 26 Trench (22 HE) } Cration group.	
		4 p.m.	(30 HE)	
			Relief of 7th Inf Bde by 50th Inf Bde was completed during the night.	
	3/8/15	During the day	The Batteries shelled important points behind German Trenches. (97 Shrap.)	
		10 am	5th By. shelled 27 Register when a German mine went up near St ELOI. (7 Shrap)	
		11.30 am	6th By. shelled 29. 30 Register at req. of O.C. L.G. in Trenches (12 HE. of wh. 6 did not burst)	
		12.32 pm	4th By shelled ruined house opp. 34, suspected of being German O.P., (7 H.E. 6. Shrap.) The last H.E. fell behind our 34 Trench to the left. The lines were not good & the shooting abnormal –	
		8 p.m.	Fuze & Shrapnel bullets picked up in 38 Trench, received from 3rd D.A. – The fuze turned out to be a Portuguese fuze – fired by a Belgian By. it was set at 4400 & was therefore probably a fuze wrongly set at 4400, instead of 5400, fired against the roads at ZWARTELEEN by 4th By. – BM/244 (Secret) received from 3rd Div. Art.	C.B. APP. XXIII
	4/8/15		During the night Batteries again shelled Roads &c. & continued to do so during the day. (74 Shrap. 8 H.E.)	
		10.50 am	5th By. fired Test 27. at req. of O.C. Trench. (1 shrap)	
		10 am	1st By. registered Trench Mortar opp. 32. (1 Shrap) on his own initiative.	
		5.7 pm	1st By shelled ——— (24 H.E.) – the infantry having evacuated the Trench by arrangement. No direct hit recorded.	
		5.30 pm & 6.10 pm	} 6th By. shelled working party opp. 30 (7 HE + 17 Shrap) to prevent them constructing a communication Trench.	C.B.

Instructions regarding War Diaries and Intelligence Summaries are contained in F. S. Regs., Part II. and the Staff Manual respectively. Title Pages will be prepared in manuscript.

WAR DIARY
or
~~INTELLIGENCE~~ SUMMARY
(Erase heading not required.)

Army Form C. 2118

(62)

Place	Date	Hour	Summary of Events and Information	Remarks and references to Appendices
	4/8/15	During	the night all Batteries shelled Roads &c in their sectors (58 Shrap.)	
		7pm	B/81 fired a few rounds Shrapnel at sap head opp. ~~29~~ 27, from the post in H30.a.8.8 - but the gun platform was not sufficiently stable - During the night the howitzers were moved back into action in H24 d 5.3.	C.S.
	5/8/15		B/81 registered lodge of Chateau O4d, knocking in S. side of it.	
		During	the day Belgian Batteries shelled Roads &c in their sectors (88 Shrap)	
		1.45pm	6th Batty shelled working party, employed in digging communication trench, opp. 29 (4 Shrap.)	
		10.15pm 10.45pm 11.55pm	6th Batty - - - - - - - - - - -(2 HE 24 Shrap.)	
		During	the night Batteries shelled Roads &c in their sectors (34 Shrap.)	
		9.9pm	3rd Batty fired Test 28. (1 Shrap) - 2 mins.	
	6/8/15	1.15am	5th Batty fired Test 27 (1 Shrap) - 9 mins. <orders issued to O.C. B/81 R.F.A. in connection with BM/244 3rd Div.>	APP. XXIV
		1.am 4 am	6th Batty shelled working party, employed in digging communication Trench, opp. 29. (16 Shrap.)	
		12.45pm	B/81 registered ruined house opp. 34 & knocked it flat	C.S.
		11.45am	6th By shelled working party opp. 28 at request of O.C. Trenches (9 HE & 2 Sh)	
		11 am	5th By. shelled 2 german sapheads opp. 27 at request of O.C. Trenches (40 H.E.)	
		2. pm	B/81 shelled german sap. opp. 27. (10 HE)	
		5.52pm	6th By shelled working party near 3rd Line Trenches opp. 30 at request of O.C. Trenches (4 HE)	
		During	the day All Batteries shelled Roads &c in their sectors (71 Shrap.)	C.S.

1875 Wt. W593/826 1,000,000 4/15 J.B.C. & A. A.D.S.S./Forms/C. 2118.

Instructions regarding War Diaries and Intelligence Summaries are contained in F. S. Regs., Part II. and the Staff Manual respectively. Title Pages will be prepared in manuscript.

WAR DIARY
or
~~INTELLIGENCE SUMMARY~~
(Erase heading not required.)

Army Form C. 2118

(63)

Place	Date	Hour	Summary of Events and Information	Remarks and references to Appendices
	6/8/15	10.23pm	5th Battery fired Trt 27 at order of O.C. Trench. (5 shrap) (3 mins)	
	7/8/15	12.30am	6th Battery shelled working party opp. 29 at request of O.C. Trench. (8 HE)	
		1.25am	3rd Battery fired Trt 28 at request of O.C. Trench - 6 mins - 20 secs. (12 shrap) - delay being due to some mistake at Bde H.Q. - probably that order was given to 5th Bty Representative instead of 3rd Bty representative.	
		During the night	all Batteries shelled Roads &c in their sectors. (51 shrap.)	
	[illegible]	During the day	— —	
		10.50am	4th Battery carried out a shoot with observation by group cdr to (78 shrap.) try & get the lines parallel.	
		4pm	B/81 shelled Lodge & knocked in S. side of it. (10 HE)	
		6pm	orders received that B/81 was to engage M.G. emplacement O4 c 55 next day	
		11pm	BM 316 Received & 8th Inf. Bde operation order No. 4.	APP. XXV + XXVI
		During the night	all Batteries shelled Roads &c. (93 shrap)	
	8/8/15	11.7am	3rd Batty registered Trench 27 (21 HE 5 shrap)	
		11.30am	6th Batty shelled Roads in rear of Trenches. (25 shrap)	
		12.5pm	1st Batty registered Trench 27 (24 HE 4 shrap)	
		1.30pm	6th Batty — — (28 HE 14 shrap)	
		5.50pm	5th Batty shell HOLLEBEKE & road O.12. (15 shrap.)	
		4pm	4th Batty ~~registered~~ shelled I35.a.32 - I35.d.03 (4 HE 18 shrap.)	
		5.40pm	4th Batty registered O4 b47. (30 shrap.)	
		2pm	B/81 shelled M.G. Emplacement O5 a 55 & flattened it out. (6 HE 13 shrap)	
		11.56pm	6th By fired Trt 29 (1 shrap) - 4½ mins.	
		During the night	all Batteries shelled Roads &c in their sectors (49 shrap)	

Instructions regarding War Diaries and Intelligence Summaries are contained in F. S. Regs., Part II. and the Staff Manual respectively. Title Pages will be prepared in manuscript.

WAR DIARY
or
INTELLIGENCE SUMMARY
(Erase heading not required.)

Army Form C. 2118

(64)

Place	Date	Hour	Summary of Events and Information	Remarks and references to Appendices
	9/9/15	2.45am -3.5am	3rd 6th & 1st Batteries shelled Trench 27 (243 HE)	
		3.5am	4th Battery shelled Wood & 2nd Line Trenches 04 & 47 (80 HE)	
		3.5-3.15am	4 Batteries above mentioned shelled same targets (328 Shrap)	
		2.45am -3.15am	5th Battery searched & swept for Hostile Batteries at O5G27 & O5G55. (177 Shrapnel)	
		4.5am	4th Battery searched for hostile Batty at O5G55 (43 Shrap)	
		4.35am -5.15am	1st & 3rd Betts. shelled Roads &c in rear of lines (95 Shrap.) - orders from Div to reduce this fire - 5.15am	
		2.45am -3.15am	B/81 shelled Batteries in O5G. (99 Sh. 18 Lyd.)	
		4.38am	Report recd from 3 D.A. that German had exploded a mine opp 27 during demonstration.	
		4.50am	Batteries ordered to search roads in their sectors with salvoes of shrapnel.	
		5.5am	Order recd from 3. D.A. to reduce the searching of Roads to ordinary rate of fire (i.e. 1 Shrap occasionally) as front from ST ELOI was quiet.	
		6.5am	B/81 reported Battery F.G. firing from about O10A86 (direction obtained from a shell hole) B/81 ordered to engage this Bty. (12 rounds Lyd)	
		5.24am	Reports from F.O.O. that parapets of 27 28 & 29 badly damaged by our demonstration. Orders sent to look out for working parties.	
		8.5am 8.35am	Reports as to situation at HOOGE received from 3rd D.A.	
		11.20pm	1st Battery shelled Roads in its sector (6 Shrap.)	
		2.25pm	Report received that Enemy were bombarding HOOGE violently - orders to engage any Batteries suspected of firing.	
		3.10pm	B/81 & 1st Battery turned on to erect of hostile Batteries in O5G N of canal. 50 Lyd 9 Shrap. 100 Shrap.	CB.

1875 Wt. W593/826 1,000,000 4/15 J.B.C. & A. A.D.S.S./Forms/C. 2118.

Instructions regarding War Diaries and Intelligence Summaries are contained in F. S. Regs., Part II. and the Staff Manual respectively. Title Pages will be prepared in manuscript.

WAR DIARY
or
INTELLIGENCE SUMMARY
(Erase heading not required.)

Army Form C. 2118

(65)

Place	Date	Hour	Summary of Events and Information	Remarks and references to Appendices
	9/8/15	3.50pm	4th Bty observer reports that he suspects 3 hostile sections of being in action in I.35.c. He opened fire on them on his own initiative (100 shrap.)	
		4.5pm	5th Bty shelled hostile Bty at O4 c 82 (53 shrap.)	
		4.10pm	Report recd from 8th Bde that enemy was shelling 'Bluff' with 6" shell.	
		4.10 p	G.O.C. 8th Bde requested that arrangements might be made to shell enemy's working parties wh. would be sure to be repairing damage to Trenches 27 28 29 during night at irregular intervals.	
		4.2 pm	3rd Bty registered damaged parapet of T.28.	
		5.5pm	5th Bty shelled hostile Batteries in O5 b55 & at same time B/81 shelled Batteries in O6 a.7.5	
		4.55pm	6th Bty ~~shelled~~ registered damaged parapet of T.29	
		5.55pm	6th Bty 6th fired T&t 29. (5 mins)	
		5.6pm	6th Bty shelled 2nd line Trenches 29. 30 (15 shrap.) to catch working parties	
		5.50pm	5th Bty shelled 27 Register at request of Inf. (4 HE)	
		During ~~night~~	the Bty Batteries shelled the Roads in their sectors (75 shrap.)	
		5.55pm	Report from Divn that all was quiet - Batteries to stop firing but to remain in observation.	
		8pm	Report as to situation at HOOGE received from 3. D.A	
		8.5pm	Orders from 3. D.A. for Counter Bty measures similar to those of preceding night	
		8.25pm	Report from 3rd D.A that enemy had opened fire to N. of our front - order to open fire with counter Batteries	
		8.43pm	5th Batty opened on German Batteries in O5 b27 & O5 b55 (70 shrap.) - at same time B/81 opened on those in O6 a (20 lyddite)	
			arrangements made for shelling the breaches in the parapets as above mentioned communicated to Inf. - who were to assist with Rifle & M.G. fire.	C.B.

1875 Wt. W593/826 1,000,000 4/15 J.B.C. & A. A.D.S.S./Forms/C. 2118.

Instructions regarding War Diaries and Intelligence Summaries are contained in F. S. Regs., Part II. and the Staff Manual respectively. Title Pages will be prepared in manuscript.

WAR DIARY
or
~~INTELLIGENCE SUMMARY~~
(Erase heading not required.)

Army Form C. 2118

(66)

Place	Date	Hour	Summary of Events and Information	Remarks and references to Appendices
	9/8/15	9pm	3 Salvos by 4th 5th & 3rd as above against 2nd line 29 30. - 27 & 28 Registered	
		9.45pm	Do Do Do	
		11pm	Do Do Do	
		11.30pm	B/81 observed flashes at 05 b 55 & 06 a 57 & opened fire on the Batteries there, which immediately stopped firing	
		11.50pm	3 Salvos by 4th, 5th, & 3rd as above	
	10/8/15	1.30am	Do Do	
		2.45am	Do Do	
		9.5	5th Batty on hearing bombardment at HOOGE opened without orders on Batteries at 05 b 55 (38 Shrap.)	
		9.7am	Message recd. from 3 D.A. that violent bombardment seemed to be in progress at HOOGE	
		9.13am	Orders from 3. D.A. to open fire on counter Battery targets for 15 mins.	
		9.15am	B/81 opened on Batteries at 05 b 55 & 06 a 57	
		9.30am	5th Bty opened on — - 05 b 55 (30 Shrap.)	
	During Day		All Batteries shelled Roads &c in their sectors (3 HE 56 Shrap.)	
		10.30am	6th Batty shelled working party near 27 Trench at request of O.C. Trench (20 HE 4 Shrap)	
		2.10pm	— — — — — — (6 HE)	
		3pm	Bm 358 Recd. from Bm 8th Inf. Bde - indicating M.G. emplacements & place where Germans were busy	
		3.5pm.	arrangements made for B/81 to shell the M.G. emplacements 3rd Batty. observer reported however that he did not consider work at 04 a 44 important enough to justify shelling	APP. XXVII
		3.25pm	6th Bty. fired Test 29. - 40 secs.	
		3.40pm	5th Bty. fired Test. 27. - 2 min 5 secs.	
		2.50pm	3rd Bty fired Test 28. - 2 min 2 secs.	
		5.3pm	6th Bty shelled working party near 27 Trench as above (16 HE 20 Shrap.)	
		6.30pm	— — — — — — (8 HE. 16 Shrap.)	
		6pm	B/81 in accordance with above mentioned orders shelled 3 M.G. emplacements in 04 a opp. 29 & knocked them completely out by direct hits.	
		8pm	5th Bty. shelled 2nd line 27 Register for effect (2 HE 2 Shrap.) as working party was observed.	* 9pm. As Germans seemed to be very busy near 27, it was arranged to shell this trench occasionally during the night. 5th Bty. given orders in consequence. C.S.
		8.5pm	Positions of O.Ps. for Batteries of Group in GHQ 2nd line [illegible] sent to 3 D.A. - 1st Bty H30 d 42 & H36 a 26. 2nd Bty H30 d 7/4. 3rd Bty H30 d 42. B/81. H 36 c 69	

X

1875 Wt. W593/826 1,000,000 4/15 J.B.C. & A. A.D.S.S./Forms/C. 2118.

Instructions regarding War Diaries and Intelligence Summaries are contained in F. S. Regs., Part II. and the Staff Manual respectively. Title Pages will be prepared in manuscript.

WAR DIARY
or
~~INTELLIGENCE SUMMARY~~
(Erase heading not required.)

Army Form C. 2118

(63)

Place	Date	Hour	Summary of Events and Information	Remarks and references to Appendices
	10/8/15	During night	Batteries shelled Roads etc in their sectors. – (16 shrap.)	
		11pm	5th Bty. shelled 27 Register in accordance with above order.	See X on preceding page
	11/8/15	1.30am	Do.	
		3am	Do Do	
		1.35am	4th Bty shelled 33 & 34 Register as Reprisal at request of O.C. Trench. (12 HE)	
		4.19am	6th Bty shelled 2nd Line 30 Register as Reprisal — — — — (12 HE)	
		4.45am	– – shelled working party near 29 to prevent work. (18 HE.)	
		5.40am	– – – – – – – (4 shrap.)	C.S.
		During the day	All Batteries shelled Roads etc. (56 Shrap.)	
		8.10am	6th Bty. shelled working party near 29 to prevent work (1 shrap.)	
		9.5am	– – – – – – – – – (11 HE 1 shrap.)	
		12.5pm	– – – – – – (6 HE 6 shrap.)	
		9.20am	4th Bty shelled Batteries at I 35.c.55 (12 shrap.)	
		11.30am	– – – – – (8 shrap.)	
		7.30pm	~~After~~ 1st Bty shelled 32 Register as Reprisal for bombardment by T.M.s (40 HE)	
		7.30pm	B/81 Bty.	
		During the night	All Batteries shelled Roads etc (37 shrap.)	
		8.40pm	5th Bty. fired Point 27 (6 hyd.) – order of 3rd D.A.	
		9.45pm	1st Bty shelled 32 Register – at request of O.C. Trench. 5 HE	
		9.47pm	– – – – – – 10 HE.	
		11pm	6th Bty shelled working parties at 29. (4 HE 4 shrap.)	
	12/8/15	1am	– – – – – (4 HE 4 shrap.)	
		10am	3rd Bty shelled Chalk Pit(?) in cooperation with 3rd Siege. 40 S. 5 HE.	
		10am	B/81	
		11.30am	B/81 shelled Dugout opp. 29 supposed to be occupied by Company Cdr. 13 hyd. 1 shr. 6 hyd	
		11.55am	6th ~~fired~~ " – – – – – – – 3 HE 2 Sh.	AS

1875 Wt. W593/826 1,000,000 4/15 J.B.C. & A. A.D.S.S./Forms/C. 2118.

Instructions regarding War Diaries and Intelligence Summaries are contained in F. S. Regs., Part II. and the Staff Manual respectively. Title Pages will be prepared in manuscript.

WAR DIARY
or
~~INTELLIGENCE SUMMARY~~
(Erase heading not required.)

Army Form C. 2118

68

Place	Date	Hour	Summary of Events and Information	Remarks and references to Appendices
	12/8/15	3.32pm	5th fired Trot 27	
		3.55pm	6th shelled Dugout opp. 29 + destroyed it.	
		5.30pm	B/81 turned onto hostile Bty supposed to be at 017 a 61, which was shelling 3rd Bty. with 10.5cm shells. The Battery stopped after firing 10 rounds - one of which was blind.	
		6.5pm	1st Bty shelled T.M. opp. 32.	
		7.20pm	6th Bty — — opp. 29	
		7.25pm	4th Bty — 33 Register as Reprisal	
		7.45pm	B/81 again shelled Bty. in 017 a 6 1. which began to shell 3rd Bty again, but only fired 3 rounds.	
		9.pm	1st Bty shelled 32 Register as Reprisal.	
		During day	all Bties. shelled Roads rc (77 S.) At 5. pm one N.CO. + 2 Telephonists were wounded in 29 from a T.M. Bomb. The N. Co. died of his wounds.	
	13/8/15	12.30 am	1st — Trot 32 (1S.)	
		4.20 am	5th — Trot 27 (1S.)	
		During night	all Bties shelled Roads rc (53 S.)	
		7.21 am	6th Bty - T.M. opp. 29 } Retaliation	
		7.36 am	6th Bty. - T.M. opp. 29 }	
		During morning	All Bties shelled Roads rc 23 S.	
		2.45pm	6th Bty shelled Working party opp. 30 to prevent them working (10 HE 8 Sh.)	
		3.15pm	4th Bty fired Trot 33.	
		3.30pm	3rd Bty. shelled behind 2e Register. in neighbourhood of German dugouts which were being shelled by 3rd Siege. (24 Sh)	
		5.30pm	3rd Bty. again fired 24 Sh. as above.	CB
		6.40pm	1st Bty fired Trot. 32 (1 shrap.)	

1875 Wt. W593/826 1,000,000 4/15 J.B.C. & A. A.D.S.S./Forms/C. 2118.

Instructions regarding War Diaries and Intelligence Summaries are contained in F. S. Regs., Part II. and the Staff Manual respectively. Title Pages will be prepared in manuscript.

WAR DIARY
or
~~INTELLIGENCE SUMMARY~~
(Erase heading not required.)

Army Form C. 2118

(69)

Place	Date	Hour	Summary of Events and Information	Remarks and references to Appendices
	14/8/15	During day	Btes shelled Roads &c (56 Shrap.)	
		3.37pm	5th Bty shelled Trench 27 (Sh.)	
		4pm	5th Bty shelled park of Chateau O4d in cooperation with 8" How. (30 S.)	
		5.50pm	5th Bty shelled park do do do (59 S.)	
		6pm	B/81 endeavoured to knock out T.Ms. situated opp. 32 (71. 16 S.)	
		6.5pm	1st Bty " " " "	
		7.30pm	B/81 " " " " (28 H.E.) – unsatisfactory shoots. Shelled Battery O17a61 – suspected of being Battery which was shelling 3rd Belgian – about 8 rounds H.E. (probably 6") fell on the dug outs lately occupied by Bdes. of 17th Divn. S. of Chateau H23b.	
		During night	Btes. shelled Roads &c	
	15/8/15	3.15am	3rd Bty fired Trench 28	
		~~3.50am~~	~~1st Bty fired~~	
		4.27am	1st Bty fired Trench 27	
		10am	3rd Bty shelled pts in Trenches in O4a – at same time as 3rd Siege Bty. (32 S.)	
		10.35am 10.36am	1st Bty fired Trench 32 & 31.	
		~~2.40pm~~	~~[illegible]~~	
		2.50pm	6th Bty shelled 2nd Bde line Trenches opp. 30 (16 H.E.)	
		3.32pm	1st Bty shelled working party opp. 31. (8 S.)	
		6.30pm	B/81 shelled Batty in O17a61. – Counter Battery – as this Battery was again shelling dug outs in H23b. (23 S.)	
		7pm	4th Bty shelled 33 Register (27 HE) as Reprisal.	
		8.20pm	1st Bty shelled T.M. opp. 32 (6 HE) Do	
		8.27pm	Do Do Do (6 HE) Do	
		8.33pm	Do Do Do Do Do	
		8.55pm	Do Do Do (12 HE) Do.	WS

Instructions regarding War Diaries and Intelligence Summaries are contained in F. S. Regs., Part II. and the Staff Manual respectively. Title Pages will be prepared in manuscript.

WAR DIARY
or
~~INTELLIGENCE SUMMARY~~
(Erase heading not required.)

Army Form C. 2118

(70)

Place	Date	Hour	Summary of Events and Information	Remarks and references to Appendices
	15/8/15	During Day	All Btrs shelled Roads &c (56 S)	
	16/8/15	12.55pm	1st Bty shelled German T.M. opp. 32 (Reprisal) 6 HE	
		1.36pm	Do Do Do 6 HE	
		1.39pm	Do Do Do 12 HE	
		5.45pm	B/81 Bty shelled group of 5 or 6 T.Ms opp. 32 (50 yds) Short very accurate enemy head shooting. Observation was from the BLUFF. Enemy must have seen the periscopes & commenced to shell BLUFF shortly after the shoot began.	
		8.32pm	1st Battery fired Test 32. (2 mins. 10")	
		9.38pm	1st Battery shelled T.Ms opp. 32. (Reprisal) 29 HE	
		During 24 hrs.	All Btrs shelled Roads &c (98 Shrap.)	
	17/8/15	9.15am	2nd Battery (which belonged to left group 17th D.A.) joined up to 6th Bty O.P. on BLUFF shelled German working party seen in O 9 b (40 S.) & dispersed it causing numerous casualties.	
		2.5pm	1st Battery - joined up to 6th Bty O.P. on BLUFF - shelled the T. Ms. opp. 32. (96 HE) with apparently good effect. after this shoot, the Bty turned on to German 1st & 2nd Line Parapets & damaged them - giving Snipers a good opportunity.	
			BM/505 - reference probable changes on the 3rd Div. & 6th Div. front received.	
		7pm	Germans shelled YPRES-VLAMERTINGHE road heavily - using gas shells	
		During 24 hrs	All Btrs. shelled Roads &c. (91 S.)	← App XXVIII
	18/8/15	3.30am	5th Bty. fired Test 27. (6 mins)	
		3.55am	3rd Bty fired Test 28. (1 min)	
			B.a/186 Col. Deckers's views on 'Test' sent to 8th Inf Bde. - Reply of G.O.C. 8th Bde recd.	App. XXIX

Wt. W593/826 1,000,000 4/15 J.B.C. & A. A.D.S.S./Forms/C. 2118.

Instructions regarding War Diaries and Intelligence Summaries are contained in F. S. Regs., Part II. and the Staff Manual respectively. Title Pages will be prepared in manuscript.

WAR DIARY
or
~~INTELLIGENCE SUMMARY~~
(Erase heading not required.)

Army Form C. 2118

(71)

Place	Date	Hour	Summary of Events and Information	Remarks and references to Appendices
	18/6/15	1.30pm	3rd D.A. O.O. on 3rd Div. O.P. No 26 Recd.	APP XXX
		6.5 pm	4th Bty shelled a German Bty at I 35 c 35 (13 S.) Counter Bty. at order of O.C. group.	
		6.35 pm	– shelled a dug out at I 34 b 62 (28 HE) at request of O.C. Trench	
		7.25pm	5th Bty & 7th/81 opened on a German Bty reported by 3rd D.A. to be firing from O 11 b 9.5 (40 S & 20 lyd respectively)	C.B.
		10.10pm	4th Bty shelled 33 Register (Reprisals) 4 HE	
		10.20pm	" " " " 20 HE	
		10.40pm	"	
		10.50pm	" shelled T.M. opp 32. 1 HE	
		10.55pm	" " " "	
		11.7pm	" " " "	
		11.10pm	" " " "	
		During 24 hrs	All Btys shelled Roads &c (68 S.)	
	19/6/15	3.20am	3rd Bty fired Test 28 (1 S)	
		3.40 am	5th Bty fired Test 27 (1 S)	
		11.40am	4th Bty registered opp. Trench 35 (1 HE 10 S)	C.S.
		12 md	6th Bty registered opp Trench 31 (10 HE)	
		10.30pm	4th Bty shelled 33 Register as Reprisal (5 HE)	
		10.30pm	1st Bty shelled T.Ms. opp 32 (18 HE)	
		9.45pm	R.A. 617 from 46th Div Art. received. stating that Dickson's group & 8th Inf. Bde passed under orders of G.O.C. 46th Divn from 7 pm	
		During 24 hrs.	All Btys shelled Roads &c (90 S)	
	20th	3.40am	3rd Bty fired Test 28 (1 S.)	
		3.50am	5th Bty fired Test 27 (1 S.)	

1875 Wt. W593/826 1,000,000 4/15 J.B.C. & A. A.D.S.S./Forms/C. 2118.

Instructions regarding War Diaries and Intelligence Summaries are contained in F. S. Regs., Part II. and the Staff Manual respectively. Title Pages will be prepared in manuscript.

WAR DIARY
or
~~INTELLIGENCE SUMMARY~~
(Erase heading not required.)

Army Form C. 2118

(72)

Place	Date	Hour	Summary of Events and Information	Remarks and references to Appendices
	20/8/15	11.25am	4th Bty shelled armoured Train at I 33 b 8/2 which was thought to be shelling our group H.Q. (20 HE 20 Sh.)	
		11.30am	6th Bty shelled working parties I 35 c 35 (6 HE & 8 S) & put them to flight.	
		12.15pm	6th Bty shelled M.G. emplacement 04a108 (41 HE)	
		3.10pm	4th Bty shelled working parties I35 b35 (12 HE 9 S.)	
		3.37pm	5th Bty shelled working parties opp. 27 (6 S.)	
		8.25pm	6th Bty shelled a Batty at 04d44 reported to be firing by R.F.C. through 2nd Group H.A.R. (20 HE & 20 S.)	
		8.45pm	1st Bty fired Test 32 (15 Sh.) (1 min 3/4").	
		9pm	Orders received renaming Dickebusch Group - Right Group - 46th D.A. - & 1 Bty to establish a line with left group 17th D.A. for use in emergency	
		During 24 hrs	All Btys shelled Roads &c (59 S)	
		9pm	Order received to exchange all Belgian (Blue) HE for French (Red & yellow) HE.	
	21/8/15	3.3 a.m	5th Batty fired Test 27 (13) - (2 mins)	A.S. APP XXXI & XXXII
		3.50am	3rd Batty fired Test 28 (13) - (1 min)	
		4.3 am	6th Batty shelled working party behind 27 (6 S.)	
		1.30pm	5th Batty shelled a German work in 1st line trench at 03 b 10.2.5 (14 HE) by arrangement with 8th Bde who evacuated the trenches. The shoot was very effective.	
		1 pm	3rd Batty shelled German ~~[illegible]~~ dugouts at 04a43 (38 HE & 9 Shrap.) with good effect.	
		2pm	B/81 shelled group of dugouts at 04a55 (40 lyd) - the dugouts were shaken in several places.	
		2.15pm	B/81 shelled German work at 04a 2.1. (40 lyd) - the excavation was damaged & an explosion caused.	
		2pm	3rd Batty fired some trial rounds with new French H.E. (13 HE)	
		2.7pm	5th Batty registered C.Ts. behind 27 Register, in order to enable to fire on them at night.	A.S.
		4.46pm	4th Batty shelled armoured Train at I 35 b 82 (8 HE & 4 Shrap.) as Counter Bty.	
		5.20pm	6th Bty registered 2nd line trench opp. 30 (15 HE & 6 Shrap). 6.58pm 1st Bty fired Test 28 (4 Shrap.)	
		9.6pm	5th Bty shelled crossroads 04c44 where German Transport was heard. (40 S.) 10.52pm 5th Bty fired Test 27.	
		11.30pm	B/81 shelled 2nd line opp. 28 (12 lyd) as Reprisal	
		11.7pm	5th & 3rd Btys shelled 27 & 28 Registers (32 HE & 103 Shrap. respectively) as reprisals. -	
		During 24 hrs	All Btys shelled Roads &c in their sectors (63 Shrap.)	
		5 pm.	R.F.C. established a wireless mast at Group H.Qs H23 b - for purpose of registering Btys with aeroplane. Operation order No 14 by G.O.C. 139th Inf. Bde & operation order No. 12 by G.O.C. R.A. 46th Div. issued.	A.S. APP XXXIII & XXXIV

1875 Wt. W593/826 1,000,000 4/15 J.B.C. & A. A.D.S.S./Forms/C. 2118.

Instructions regarding War Diaries and Intelligence Summaries are contained in F. S. Regs., Part II. and the Staff Manual respectively. Title Pages will be prepared in manuscript.

WAR DIARY
or
~~INTELLIGENCE SUMMARY~~
(Erase heading not required.)

Army Form C. 2118

(73)

Place	Date	Hour	Summary of Events and Information	Remarks and references to Appendices
	22/8/15	2.30 am	5th Bty shelled Crossroads 04c44 (40 Shrap.) where German ~~Trans~~ Transport had been heard.	
		9.50 am	4th Bty fired some trial rounds with new HE. (16 HE)	
		11.55 am	4th Bty shelled a German O.P. at I 35 a 82 (21 HE)	
		1.58 pm	4th Bty — — — — (12 HE)	
		12.30 pm - 2.25 pm	5th Bty registered 04d44. 04d99 04c53 05a00. with aeroplane observation (3 HE 44 Shrap.)	
		1.50 pm	6th Bty fired some trial rounds with new HE (12 HE) on 29 & 28 Registers —	
		2.45 pm	4th Bty registered Trenches 33.34.35 with new HE (9 HE)	
		3.20 pm	3rd Bty — — 28 with new HE (23 HE)	
		4.45 pm	5th Bty shelled 2nd line Trench opp. 29 as Reprisal (24 HE)	
		5.10 pm	3rd Bty shelled — — — 28 — (28 HE)	
		5.25 pm	4th Bty shelled armoured Train (4 HE 2 Shrap) at I 35 ~~b~~ 6.8.2.	
		6.30 pm	3rd Bty shelled CTs behind Trench 28 as Reprisal (30 Shrap.)	
		6.43 pm	5th Bty — — — 27 — — (30 Shrap.)	
		6.43 pm	6th Bty — 2nd line Trench opp. 29 — (30 Shrap.)	
		4.40 pm	B/81 shelled — — — 28 — — (8 Lyddite)	
		During night	All Btys shelled Roads &c in their sectors (40 Shrapnel) — 5.20 pm Inf. Brought down an (German) aeroplane. It fell behind German lines. according to Observer behind 28. Register —	
	23/8/15	3.30 am	3rd Bty fired Test 28.	
		3.40 am	5th Bty fired Test 27	
		9 am	2nd Bty (Left Group 17th D.A.) reported the discovery of posn of German Bty (or gun) shelling KRUISSTRAAT Cross-roads at O10b77	
		12 midday	2nd Bty reports that this Bty is firing	
		12.5 pm	3rd Bty opened fire on it (40 HE & 40 Shrap.) as Counter Bty. O.C. 91st H. Bde. also engaged it with his 4.7s.	
		2.50 pm	6th Bty shelled M.G. in trench opp. 29 (1 Sh. & 8 HE)	
		3.6 pm	German heavy gun at O10b77 again opened as 5th Bty shelled it (40 Sh. + 20 HE)	
		12 mn.	Report Received that Relief of 8th by 139th Inf Bde was complete	
		12.55 am	3rd Bty. shelled German work at 04a23 which had already been taken on in the afternoon by 6" Howitzers. (43 Shrap. 30 HE)	
		During night	The German replied by firing a few Shrapnel at Trenches 27 & 28 — . All Btys shelled Roads &c in their Sectors (58 Shrap.)	
	24/8/15	9 am	Autograph letter from G.O.C. 3rd Divn received thanking Col. Drake for the work of his Regt.	

Initials in Remarks column: A.S. (beside 23/8/15 entries); C.S.; C.B.; C.B.

Instructions regarding War Diaries and Intelligence Summaries are contained in F. S. Regs., Part II. and the Staff Manual respectively. Title Pages will be prepared in manuscript.

WAR DIARY
or
~~INTELLIGENCE SUMMARY~~
(Erase heading not required.)

Army Form C. 2118

(74)

Place	Date	Hour	Summary of Events and Information	Remarks and references to Appendices
	24/8/15	3.15 pm, 3.45 pm, 4.7 pm, 4.20 pm	6th Bty. Shelled working party opp. 31. 130 (8 HE 6 Shrap) at request of Inf	
		4.55 pm	4th Bty shelled Bty at I 35 d 83 as Counter Bty. (40 Shrap.)	
		6.45 pm	4th Bty — — — I 35 d 83 — — — (20 HE 40 Sh.)	
		During Day	All Btys shelled Roads &c (65 Shrap.)	
	25/8/15	12 mn	3rd Bty shelled Register 28 (9 Sh.) as Reprisals at request of Inf.	
		12.10 am	5th Bty — — 27 (24 Sh.) as Reprisals at request of Inf.	
		12.13 am	5th Bty fired Test 27 (1 Sh)	
		2.30 am	3rd Bty shelled destroyed German work at O 4 a 2 3 at request of Inf. (40 HE 20 Shrap.)	
		During night	All Btys shelled Roads &c (11 Shrap.)	
		2.20 pm	3rd Bty. fired Test 28. (1 Sh.)	
		2.35 pm	3rd Bty. shelled working party O 4 b 9.2. (11 Shrap.)	
		3.59 pm	1st Bty. fired Test 32. (1 Sh.)	
		6 pm	5th Bty. registered antiaircraft Bty at O 11 b 95 with aeroplane observation (16 Sh.)	
		6.15 pm	B/81 — — — — — — (16 Sh.)	
		3.15 pm	6th Bty. registered with new HE + on targets to left of its Zone with Shrapnel (3 Sh.)	A.S.
		7 25 pm	1st Bty. shelled a T.M. opposite 32 (10 HE) at request of Inf (20 HE + 12 Sh.)	
		During night	All Btys shelled Roads &c (58 Shrap)	
	26/8/15	3.35 am	5th Bty fired Test 27 (1 Shrap)	
		5 am	3rd Bty. shelled German transport heard at I 34 d 8 0 (5 Shrap.)	
		12.15 pm	4th Bty Shelled 34 Register as Reprisal (16 HE)	
		12.27 pm	6th Bty. fired Test 30 (2 Sh.)	
		2 29 pm	6th Bty shelled 29 Register (20 HE) Reprisal	
		2 29 pm	3rd Bty shelled 28 Register (20 HE) Reprisal	A.S.

1875. Wt. W593/826 1,000,000 4/15 J.B.C. & A. A.D.S.S./Forms/C. 2118.

Instructions regarding War Diaries and Intelligence Summaries are contained in F. S. Regs., Part II. and the Staff Manual respectively. Title Pages will be prepared in manuscript.

WAR DIARY
or
INTELLIGENCE SUMMARY
(Erase heading not required.)

Army Form C. 2118

(75)

Place	Date	Hour	Summary of Events and Information	Remarks and references to Appendices
	26/6/15	2.30pm	B/81 shelled 29 Register as Reprisal (12 Lyd) – Enemy shelling Bluff.	
		4.33pm	5th Bty fired Tact 27 ~~[illegible]~~ (1 Shrap)	
		5.50pm	1st Bty fired Tact 32 (1 Shrap)	
		During day	All Btys shelled Roads &c in their Sectors (57 Shrap)	
		10.3pm, 10.39pm, 11.17pm, 11.25pm, 11.37pm, 11.40pm, 11.43pm	6th Bty fired Tact 30 (7 Shrap.)	
		11.10pm	1st Bty fired Tact 32 (1 Shrap)	GB
	27/6/15	12.10am	3rd Bty fired Tact 28	
		3.22am	5th Bty fired Tact 27	
		During night	Btys shelled Roads &c (11 Shrap.)	
		6.35am	5th Bty shelled pts. 04c53 + 010b36 as Transport was heard there (8 Shrap.)	
		7.25am	1st Bty shelled 31 Register (2 Shrap)	
		7.35am	1st Bty — — — (2 Shrap)	
		10.30am	6th Bty shelled Bty at 010c93 suspected of shelling 3rd Bty + Inf Dugouts in Rear. (6 Shrap)	
		11.21am	B/81 shelled Bty at 017a81 — — — — (8 Lyd)	
		11.40am	B/81 — — — — — — (8 Lyd) Hostile fire ceased.	
		11.30am	6th Bty fired Tact 30 (1 Shrap.)	
		1.5pm	3rd Bty fired Tact 28 (1 Shrap.)	
		1.35pm	B/81 Registered following pts. with aeroplane observation 011b95, 010b65, 010d83, 09b24 (5 Lyd 8 Shrap)	
		2pm	4th Bty shelled 34 Register (11 HE) as Reprisal	
		3.25pm	B/81 again shelled Bty 017a61 suspected of shelling Inf. Dugouts in rear of 3rd Bty	GB

Army Form C. 2118

(76)

Instructions regarding War Diaries and Intelligence Summaries are contained in F. S. Regs., Part II. and the Staff Manual respectively. Title Pages will be prepared in manuscript.

WAR DIARY
or
~~INTELLIGENCE SUMMARY~~
(Erase heading not required.)

Place	Date	Hour	Summary of Events and Information	Remarks and references to Appendices
	27/8/15	5.20pm	4th Bty shelled 34 Register (26 HE 75 Shrap) as Reprisal for Trench Mortars.	
		5.25pm	3rd Bty shelled a German Bty at O4 d 68 as complaint was received from 17th Divn that the S.F. S/01 trenches were being shelled from this direction. (40 HE & 20 Shrap.)	
		5.25pm	1st Bty shelled German Trench Mortars opposite Trench 32. as Reprisal (30 HE)	
		5.30pm	5th Bty shelled German Bty at O 4 b 55 in response to above request of 17th Divn (20 HE 20 Shrap)	
		6.15pm	1st Bty shelled T.M. opp. 32. (18 HE)	
		6.32pm	1st Bty — — — — (6 HE)	
		6.50pm	6th Bty shelled 29-30 Register (26 HE)	
		9.5pm	3rd Bty shelled 28 Register (16 Shrap) as Reprisal.	
		11.10pm	6th Bty shelled 29.30 Register (11 HE) (17 Shrap)	
		During day	All Btys shelled Roads &c in their sectors (67 Shrap)	C.S.
	28/8/15	12.15am	6th Bty shelled 29-30 Register (6 HE 1 Shrap)	
		3.30am	5th Bty fired Test 27 (1 Shrap.)	
		6.30am	3rd Bty shelled German Transport behind HOLLEBEKE CHATEAU (4 Shrap)	
		9.35am	6th Bty verified Registration at side of B.C in Trenches (2 HE 2 Shrap)	
		9.30am	2 men of 6th Bty were wounded by a shell which fell in rear of Bty on DICKEBUSCH Road	C.S.
		2.39pm	3rd Bty fired Test 28 (1 Shrap.)	
		4.20pm	5th Bty fired Test 27 (1 Shrap.)	
		6.15pm	6th Bty shelled 29 Register as Reprisal (4 HE.)	
		6.20pm	1st Bty shelled 32 Register as Reprisal (24 HE)	
		7.33pm	3rd Bty shelled 28 Register as Reprisal (4 Shrap)	
		8. pm 8.2 pm 8.4 pm	6th Bty fired Test 30 (1 Shrap)	
		8.10pm	3rd Bty shelled 28 Register as Reprisal (8 Shrap)	

1875 Wt. W593/826 1,000,000 4/15 J.B.C. & A. A.D.S.S./Forms/C. 2118.

Instructions regarding War Diaries and Intelligence Summaries are contained in F. S. Regs., Part II. and the Staff Manual respectively. Title Pages will be prepared in manuscript.

WAR DIARY
or
~~INTELLIGENCE SUMMARY~~
(Erase heading not required.)

Army Form C. 2118.

(77)

Place	Date	Hour	Summary of Events and Information	Remarks and references to Appendices
	28/8/15	9.47 pm	6th Bty fired Test 30. (1 Shrap)	
		11.30 pm	1st Bty fired Test 32. (1 Shrap)	
		11.52 pm	6th Bty fired Test 30. (1 Shrap)	
			B/81 has registered mound at St Eloi.	
	29/8/15	1.49 am	3rd Bty fired Test 28 (1 Shrap)	
		7.50 am	1st Bty shelled working party opposite 32 (7 Shrap)	
		9.20 am	4th Bty shelled 34 register as reprisal (32 H.E.)	
		9.30 am	6th Bty shelled 2nd line Trench opposite 30 as reprisal (20 Shrap)	
		9.40 am	1st Bty shelled working party opposite 32 (35 Shrap)	
		9.42 am	1st Bty shelled 32 register as reprisal (20 H.E.)	
		9.50 am	1st Bty shelled 32 register as reprisal (16 H.E.)	
		11.40 am	1st Bty - registration (3 H.E.)	
		12.5 pm	B/81 shelled 32 register as reprisal (6 H.E.)	
		4.45 pm	5th Bty shelled road O.11 (2 Shrap)	
		5.59 pm	5th Bty shelled Hollebeke (2 Shrap)	
		6.33 pm	5th Bty shelled road O11 (2 Shrap)	
		6.58 pm	5th Bty " " (2 Shrap)	
		7.15 pm	4th Bty shelled 34 register as reprisal (12 H.E.)	
		7.42 pm	5th Bty shelled Hollebeke (2 Shrap)	
		9.15 pm	6th Bty fired Test 29 Register (1 Shrap)	
	30/8/15	2.55 am	5th Bty fired Test 27 Register (1 Shrap)	
		7. am - 12.50 pm	5th Bty shelled Hollebeke (7 Shrap)	
		9.50 am	1st Bty shelled working party 32 Register (4 Shrap)	
		1. pm	4th Bty shelled armoured train (7 H.E. 6 Shrap)	
		1.57 pm	6th Bty fired Test 30 register (1 Shrap)	
		3.40 pm	1st Bty fired ~~Test~~ on Trench Mortar 32 register as reprisal (16 H.E.)	
		11.10 pm	3rd Bty fired Test on 28 register (1 Shrap)	
	31/8/15	3.27 am	5th Bty fired Test on 27 Register (1 Shrap)	
		8.25 am	4th Bty shelled armoured train (6 Shrap)	
		9.40 am	5th Bty shelled 27 Register as reprisal (16 Shrap)	

1875 Wt. W593/826 1,000,000 4/15 J.B.C. & A. A.D.S.S./Forms/C. 2118.

Army Form C. 2118

(78)

WAR DIARY
or
~~INTELLIGENCE SUMMARY~~

(Erase heading not required.)

Instructions regarding War Diaries and Intelligence Summaries are contained in F. S. Regs., Part II. and the Staff Manual respectively. Title Pages will be prepared in manuscript.

Place	Date	Hour	Summary of Events and Information	Remarks and references to Appendices
	31/8/15	12.10 pm	4th Bty Shelled M.G. in I 35 C 6/0 (9 H.E.)	
		2.45 pm	3rd Bty fired Test 78 register (1 shrap)	
		4.25 pm	1st Bty Shelled Trench mortars as reprisal (8 H.E.)	
		5.37 pm	5th Bty Shelled Communications (2 shrap)	
		6.20 pm	1st Bty Shelled Trench mortars as reprisal (10 H.E.)	
		6.30 pm	5th Bty Shelled Communications (2 shrap)	
		6.38 pm	5th Bty " " (4 shrap)	
		7. pm	5th Bty " " (1 shrap)	
		10.20 pm	3rd Bty fired Test 78 register (1 shrap)	
		11.11 pm	6th Bty " " (1 shrap)	
				CS

1875 Wt. W593/826 1,000,000 4/15 J.B.C. & A. A.D.S.S./Forms/C. 2118.

Secret

Left Group
Centre Group
40th FA Bde.

17 Div Arty (for information
3rd Division

BM 244.

APPENDIX XXIII

Appended below is a list of enemy gun emplacements. With view to engaging these batteries, if necessary, they are allotted to batteries as indicated and will be registered upon by aeroplane on dates stated:.

	Unit.	Target	Date	Remarks
	41st Bty	O. 9. 7. 9. 1.	4th Aug.	Ground station at 130th Bty. 41st to be connected through Centre Gro
40th Bde RFA	6th Bty	O. 9. b. 3. 4 / O. 9. c. 4. 9.	5th Aug.	Ground station will be put at 40 Bde H.Q. at H. 28. d. 5. 6. by CEN Group on evening of 4/5th August 40th Bde H.Q. will then arrange send the wireless signals to the Batteries as required. A RF Officer will visit OC 40th Bde tomorrow between 2 pm & 4 pm to arrange.
	23rd Bty.	O. 10. d. 8. 9 / O. 10. d. 5. 9.	5th Aug.	
	49th Bty	O. 9. d. 0. 4	5 Aug.	

IN ADDITION

130th How Bty.	O. 15. a. 3. 1 / O. 21. b. 6. 6 / O 16 a 4. 9.	4th Aug.	All cross roads.
No 5 Belgian Bty.	O 8. b. 2. 7 / O 8. b. 5. 5.		Will not be registered thereon, but will be prepared to search these when ordered.

Exact times for the registration cannot be given, but CENTRE Group Comm and OC. 40th Bde. will arrange these as near possible with the R.F.C. officer when he calls on them.

Special for 40th Bde.

For the above purpose 40th Bde will go into action on night of 4/5th August as follows:-

6th Battery at H. 29. c. 5. 5.
23rd " H 35 b 8. 6. } Bde H Q. at H. 28. d. 5. 6.
49th " H 35 a 4. 5.

These Batteries will be employed entirely as "counter-batteries" except in emergency. They are not required to register on enemy's trenches, but will be prepared to search and sweep the roads and approaches to the enemy's lines in the areas allotted to them above if required.

Please wire receipt.

3rd August 1915
4 pm.

R. G. Finlayson Major, RA.
Bde Major R.A. 3rd Division

APP. XXIV

B.A. / 128

BMRA
3rd Divn

As no reference was made in your BM/244 d/d. 3/8/15 to B/81 How. Batty R.F.A. – the enclosed orders have been sent to this Battery to enable it to take part in any action against hostile artillery.

Charles Briggs
Capt RA
for O.C. Duchessmo Group.

5/8/15

OPP. Secret
XXIV

Operation order No. 1
by
Colonel Duchesne.

(1) There exist in O5 b a group of 7 German Batteries. Six of these Batteries are situated in a square of 200 yards side, of which the centre is at O5 b.4.7. The Range to the centre of the square from the position of B/81 Battery is about 5700 yards.

(2) O.C. B/81 Battery should be prepared to engage these Batteries by searching for them between 5500 & 5900 yards, & by opening out his lines of fire so as to cover a front of 200 yards.

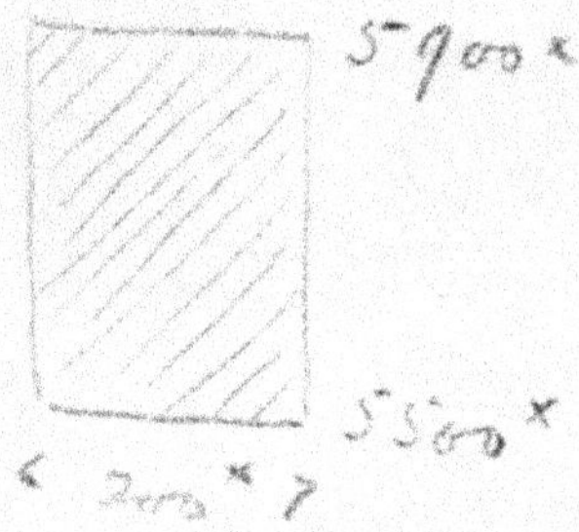

(3) Supposing that 36 rounds are available for the shoot, it should be carried out by firing salvos of 4 shrapnel, beginning at 5500 & increasing the range by 100x up to 5900 - & then diminishing by 50x, down to 5550x.

(4) O.C. B/81 Batty. should be prepared to carry out this shoot when he gets any adv.

(50)

Dickson.

Col. Cog. Group.

5/8/15

Copy No. 1. – O.C. 13/8.

Copy No. 2. 5th Da.

— No. 3. File.

"A" Form. APP. XXV

Army Form C. 2121.

MESSAGES AND SIGNALS.

No. of Message..........

Prefix ..... Code ..... m.	Words	Charge	This message is on a/c of:	Recd. at ..... m.
Office of Origin and Service Instructions. SECRET	Sent At ..... m. To ..... By		..... Service. (Signature of "Franking Officer.")	Date ..... From ..... By .....

TO
DESCHESNES Group
CENTRE [illegible]
40 Bde RFA

Sender's Number.	Day of Month.	In reply to Number	
* BM 376	7 August		AAA

It is notified for information that if, during the operations on the 9th Aug., O.C. 40th Bde receives by means of his wireless ground station any important information he will send it at once to ~~both~~ the two above mentioned groups who will act upon it at once reporting action taken to this HQ. This action, in the case of information regarding enemy's artillery firing, will be limited to the batteries already detailed as counter batteries. Action of other batteries, except in urgent cases or fleeting opportunities, which must be dealt with unhesitatingly by group commanders, will be detailed from RA HQ or by the Infantry.

From
Place
Time 10.30 pm

R.G. [illegible]
Maj. RA
38 D

The above may be forwarded as now corrected. (Z)

Censor. Signature of Addressor or person authorised to telegraph in his name.

* This line should be erased if not required.

(75644) Wt 11400/2045 30,000 2.15 B. M. & S. Ltd.

8th Bde Operation Order No 4

APP XXVI

Reference map 1/10.000. 8th August 1915

1\. The 6th Division is to attack the position about HOOGE tomorrow morning.
One Brigade attacks from SANCTUARY WOOD, and another attacks North of the MENIN road.
The Artillery preparation will begin at 2.45 am and the Infantry assault will take place at 3.15 am.

2\. 8th Bde will, with the assistance of 4 Belgian batteries and a forward gun of 41st Battery R.F.A. carry out a demonstration South of the Canal with a view to misleading the Enemy and, if possible, drawing the fire of his guns.

3\. The Belgian batteries and the forward gun mentioned above will bombard the enemy's trenches S. of the canal from 2.45 am to 3.15 am.

4\. O.C. No 40 Trench Howitzer Battery will fire from the S. bank of the Canal between above hours.

5\. O.C. 2nd Suffolk Regt will have his fire trenches cleared between O.3.b.7.3 and O.3.b.10.5, also his support trenches between O.3.b.6.4 and O.3.b.9.6 during the bombardment.
The garrisons of trenches 27 F & S and 28 F & S should be reduced to about 12 men in each trench besides Machine Guns during the period of the bombardment.

6\. The B.M.G.O. will arrange to have all available trench howitzers in action, and will have 2 Machine Guns in position ready to open fire on any target that offers.

7\. From 2.45 am until the front has become quiet all troops should remain in the vicinity of their dug-outs.

8\. O.C. 2nd Suffolk Regt and 4th Gordon Highrs will have all snipers in action during the bombardment. Troops in trenches will be ready to seize any opportunity of opening fire that may be presented.

9\. Acknowledge

H.P. Burn

Bde Major,
8th Infantry Bde

Copies to:-
All Battalions
40th Trench How: Battery.
Dechesne's Group.

"A" Form. Army Form C. 2121.

MESSAGES AND SIGNALS. No. of Message

Prefix	Code	m.	Words	Charge	This message is on a/c of:	Recd. at	m.
Office of Origin and Service Instructions			Sent		App. XXVII Service	Date	
			At	m.		From	
			To				
			By		(Signature of "Franking Officer.")	By	

TO DECHESNES GROUP

Sender's Number	Day of Month	In reply to Number	AAA
* BM358	10th		

Suffolks report German machine gun emplacements as follows:—

No. 1. 15 yds North of water of canal in German front line.

No. 2. in support line just behind No 1.

No 3 half-way up bank on N. side of canal facing towards trench 28.

Suffolks can supply an Officer who can point out these & other suspected emplacements to F.O.O.

Perhaps B/81 could deal with above when it may be convenient to you to do so.

From

Place

Time

(PTO)

The above may be forwarded as now corrected. (Z)

Censor. Signature of Addressor or person authorised to telegraph in his name.

* This line should be erased if not required.

(15491) S. & Co. Ltd. W 14142/641. 90,000. 4/15. Forms C 2121/10.

"A" Form. Army Form C. 2121.

MESSAGES AND SIGNALS. No. of Message

Prefix Code m. | Words | Charge | This message is on a/c of: Service. (Signature of "Franking Officer.") | Recd. at m. Date From By

Office of Origin and Service Instructions

2

Sent At m. To By

TO

Sender's Number	Day of Month	In reply to Number	AAA
*BM358 (contd)			

4 Gordon Hrs report Germans busy at work during last few days at O 4 a Hill. A good deal of work done here last night.

H. P. Buller Bde Major
8 Bde

From
Place
Time

The above may be forwarded as now corrected. (Z)

Censor. Signature of Addressor or person authorised to telegraph in his name.

* This line should be erased if not required.

(15191) S. & Co. Ltd. W 14142/641. 90,000. 4/15. Forms C 2121/10.

"A" Form. APP. XXVIII Army Form C. 2121.

MESSAGES AND SIGNALS.

No. of Message

Prefix ... Code ... m.	Words	Charge	This message is on a/c of:	Recd. at
Office of Origin and Service Instructions	Sent		Service.	Date
SECRET	At ... m.			From
	To			By
	By		(Signature of "Franking Officer.")	

TO: Dechesnes Group. ~~30th Bde~~
~~23 Bde~~ . ~~42nd Bde.~~
~~40 Bde~~ .

Sender's Number	Day of Month	In reply to Number	AAA
* BM 505	17 Aug.		

It is notified for information that the following moves are in contemplation. Approximate dates & fronts only are given herein as a preliminary notice.

Night 18/19 & 19/20. 9th Inf. Bde relieves 139th I.B. from I.30.b.2.4 to J.13.c.1.4, & this front & RA covering it (23rd Bde & 129th Bde) come under 3 Divn on night of 19/20.

Night 19/20. 8th Inf Bde & Dechesnes group to come under 46th Divn

Night 24/25. 8th Inf Bde, which will have been withdrawn, takes over from 6th Divn the front from left of 9th I.B. to I.18.a.4.10.

Night of 25/26, 27/28 – 40th or 42nd Bde (probably former) takes over from the bde at present covering the HOOGE front, covers 8th I.B. 130th Bty to come into action near YPRES & do likewise.

7th Inf Bde will eventually relieve 8th I.B.

From RA. HQ. will remain here. An exchange will be
Place established somewhere near KRUISSTRAAT.
Time

The above may be forwarded as now corrected. (Z) R.G. [illegible] Maj. BM

Censor. Signature of Addressor or person authorised to telegraph in his name.

* This line should be erased if not required.

(15491) S. & Co. Ltd. W 14142/641. 90,000. 4/15. Forms C 2121/10.

APP XXIX

O.C. Deckesne's Group

I quite concur with Your D.A. 186.

If we are satisfied that the Standard which Colonel Deckesne lays down has been attained, it will not be necessary to carry out Tests except at irregular intervals.

The personnel of the Belgian Artillery is very small, so the communications and system have to be of the best, if the desired result is to be gained.

Perhaps Colonel Deckesne agrees with me in thinking that it is necessary for the Artillery themselves to carry out the even more important tests of switching all guns off their night lines on to one particular part of the front, so as to open a concentrated fire as rapidly as possible - But this, of course, is a matter of Test by the Artillery themselves.

A.J. Hoskin Brig. General
Comd 5th Brigade

18/8/15

Defence Proj.

APP XXX

3rd Divisional Artillery Operation Order

SECRET

(on 3rd Division O.O. No.26.)

Ref: 1/20000 Sheet 28. Copy No. 9

18th August, 1915.

1. At 7 p.m. on August 19th the 8th Inf. Bde and Artillery now covering 8th Inf. Bde front namely 7th Belgian Regt. Artillery (less 1 Battery), B/81 How; Btty - 1 section 3rd Siege Batty - and No 40 Trench How. Batty. will come under orders of 46th Division.

2. (a) On night 19th/20th August 9th Inf Bde will relieve 139th Inf Bde of 46th Division on front about I.24.d.7.0. to junction with VI Corps J.13.c.1.6.
(b) On night of 20th/21st August 9th Inf Bde will extend its right to about I.30.b.2.5. relieving a portion of 139th Inf Bde.
Commands of fronts relieved to pass from 46th Division to 3rd Division from hour of completion of each relief.
At same hours artillery covering front relieved will come under orders of 3rd Division; namely after relief (A) 23rd Bde R.F.A., 129th How; Batty R.F.A., 5th Staffs Batty R.F.A., 1 section Naval Anti-aircraft Guns, and No 20 Trench How. Batty; after relief (B) 6th North Staffs Batty.

3. The grouping of the R.A. under O.C. 23rd F.A. Bde will remain as at present; 23rd Bde will be connected by R.A. Signals to this H.Q., and will connect his own H.Q. to that of 9th Inf Bde.
After completion of relief on night 20/21 August the 6th North Staffs Battery will come under the group of O.C. 23rd Bde, for the present. O.C. 23rd Bde will arrange the necessary communications, receiving assistance from Signals 3rd D.A.

4. From completion of reliefs mentioned in para (2) boundary for purposes of defence between 3rd and 46th Divisions will run from point of junction in front line to road junction I.24.c.9.3., thence Westwards along south side of road, South of Zillebeke Village to S.E. corner of Zillebeke Pond (defences of Zillebeke to 3rd Division) thence along S.Bank of Lake to bend in road I.21.a.5.5. along road I.20.a.6.3. (road to 46th Division) thence to Canal I.19.d.7.3. (defences of canal to 46th Division).

5. Bridges on the Lys canal 19 to 12 inclusive will be allotted for protection and maintenance to 9th Inf Bde from 7 a.m. on 20th.
Arrangements for demolition to be made by C.R.E. 3rd Division.

6. This H.Q. remains as at present; 23rd Bde will report by telephone at 7 p.m. on 19th and on completion of reliefs on night 20th/21st as to whether all communications are correct.

7. Acknowledge.

ISSUED AT 12 NOON.

R.G. [signature] Major R.A.
Brigade Major 3rd Divisional Arty.

App XXXI

DIVISIONAL ARTILLERY ORDERS,

By Brigadier General Herbert M. Campbell,

Commanding 46th: Divisional Artillery.

NO ORDERS WERE ISSUED ON THE 19th: AUGUST, 1915.

Command:-

233. RENAMING OF GROUPS

From 6 p.m. tonight, Artillery Groups of the Division will be re-named as follows:-

RIGHT GROUP - DESCHESNE'S Group consisting of 7th: Belgian Regiment (Less 1 Battery) and B/81 Howitzer Battery, under Command of O.C. Deschesne's Group.

CENTRE GROUP- 2nd: North Midland Brigade. R.F.A. and 1st: Lincs: Battery, under Command of O.C. 2nd: North Midland Brigade. R.F.A.

LEFT GROUP - 2nd: Lincs:, 3rd: Lincs:, and 4th: Staffs: Batteries under Command of O.C. 3rd: North Midland Brigade. R.F.A.

W.A.S. Stirling Captain R.A.

for Brigade Major.

46th: Divisional Artillery.

H.Q. R.A.

20th: August, 1915.

OC B/81 R.F.A.

For Information & Return

Charles Bridge
Capt R.A.
for OC Right Group

2.

The O.C.

Rt Group.

Noted & returned

21/6/15.

T. Fulton Major R.A.

Comdg B/81 1st Bde R.F.A.

APP XXXII

C.R.A.
No. 630
Date
46th (N.M.) DIV.

Subject:- Communication. Zones to be covered.

O.C. Deschesne's Group.

Please instruct O.C. B/81 Battery to run a wire to Headquarters, Left Group, 17th: Division.

In addition to covering his present Zone, he will be at the disposal of the 17th: Divisional Artillery when required, and will if necessary, alter his Emplacements so as to allow his guns to switch, and cover the Mound and Q.1 Trench inclusive.

[signature] Captain R.A.
for Brigade Major.
46th: Divisional Artillery.

H.Q. R.A.
20th: August, 1915.

O.C. B/81st Bde R.F.A.

Forwarded to you for information, necessary action & return please. Further instructions as to ammn allotment will be sent you.

Charles Briggs
Capt R.A.
for O.C. Right Group

2

The O.C.
B/81st Bde R.F.A.

Noted & returned.
The present position of my guns are suitable for this switch.

T. Sutton Major RA
Comdg. B/81st Bde R.F.A.

21/8/15.

APP. XXXIII

Ref.Map.BELGIUM.
Sheet 28.1/40,000

Copy No. 11

OPERATION ORDER. No. 14
- by -
BRIGADIER GENERAL C.T.SHIPLEY.
Commanding 139th Infantry Brigade.

August 21/15

1. The 139th Infantry Brigade will take over the Trench Line at present occupied by the 8th Infantry Brigade on the night of the 23/24th instant as follows :-

(a) The 6th Battalion Sherwood Foresters will relieve the 2nd Battalion Suffolk Regt., and the 1st Battalion Gordon Highlanders in Trenches Nos. 27, 28 and 29 with Battalion Headquarters at SPOILBANK.
These Trenches will in future be known as the RIGHT SECTOR Trenches.

(b) The 7th Battalion Sherwood Foresters will relieve the 1st Battalion Gordon Highlanders and the 1st Battalion Middlesex Regt., in Trenches Nos. 30, 31 and 32, with Headquarters in rear.
These Trenches will in future be known as the LEFT SECTOR Trenches.

(c) The 5th Battalion Sherwood Foresters will go into Support in the SPOILBANK Dug-outs and those on the North side of the Canal with Headquarters in the latter.
This Battalion will also furnish the garrison for LA CHAPELLE Strong Post.

2. Full instructions have already been issued to Officers Commanding Units concerned regarding the strength of the garrisons for the various Trenches.

3. Battalions will parade in the afternoon of the 23rd instant so as to be at Road junction H.18.c.9.0 at the following hours where Company Guides from the 8th Infantry Brigade will meet them.

6th Battalion Sherwood Foresters	7-30 p.m.
7th Battalion Sherwood Foresters	8-0 p.m.
5th Battalion Sherwood Foresters	8-30 p.m.

Further Platoon Guides will be in waiting at WOODCOTE HOUSE.

4. The Machine Guns of the 139th Infantry Brigade will relieve those of the 8th Infantry Brigade on the night of the 22/23rd instant.
These guns will parade under arrangements to be made by the Brigade Machine Gun Officer, so as to be at Road junction H,18.c. 9.0 at 7-45 p.m. on the 22nd instant, where guides from the 8th Infantry Brigade will meet them.

5. A separate memorandum is being issued with reference to the Artillery Support and Communications.

6. The Brigade Mining Section will take over all mines in the Trenches relieved and be accommodated in the dug-outs behind 32 R.Trench.

7. Dumps are adjacent to each Battalion Headquarters.

8. Officers Commanding Units will ensure that a complete List of all Trench Stores taken over is made out. These Lists will be ~~forwared~~ forwarded to the Brigade Office by noon on the 24th instant.

9. Further instructions will be issued with regard to Regimental Aid Posts.

10. Brigade Headquarters will be at WOODCOTE HOUSE (Square I.20.c.5.2) from 10 p.m. the 23rd instant.

11. Acknowledge.

W.G.NEILSON.Captain.

Brigade Major, 139th Infantry Brigade.

<u>Issued at 8 p.m. to :-</u>

Copy	No. 1.	To file (War Diary)
"	" 2.	46th Division
"	" 3.	5th Battalion Sherwood Foresters.
"	" 4.	6th " " "
"	" 5.	7th " " "
"	" 6.	8th " " "
"	" 7.	8th Infantry Brigade.
"	" 8.	137th Infantry Brigade
"	" 9.	1st N.M.F.A.
"	" 10.	No. 4 Coy. A.S.C.
"	" 11.	Deschesne's Group.
"	" 12.	Brigade Mining Officer.
"	" 13.	Brigade Machine Gun Officer.

4e Bde [illegible]

app. XXXIV
3

SECRET fol 2 COPY ....

46th: DIVISIONAL ARTILLERY OPERATION ORDER NO: 12.

(On 46th: DIVISION OPERATION ORDER NO: 14)

21st: August, 1915.

INFORMATION (1) The following reliefs will take place under arrangements made by Brigadiers concerned:-

(a) On the night of August 22nd:/23rd: the 138th: Infantry Brigade will extend to its right taking over Trench 41 (a) from 137th: Infantry Brigade.

(b) On the night of August 23rd:/24th: the 137th: Infantry Brigade will extend to its Right taking over Trenches 34 and 33, from 8th: Infantry Brigade

(c) On the night of August 23rd:/24th: the 139th: Infantry Brigade will take over from the 8th: Infantry Brigade the remainder of the front held by the latter, i.e. from Trench 27, to Trench 32, Both inclusive.

Alterations in Zones will take place on same date as Infantry Reliefs.

INSTRUCTIONS (2)

RIGHT GROUP (a)

Colonel A.E.M. Deschesne's Group of Belgian Artillery and B/81 4.5 inch Howitzer Battery R.F.A. will remain covering Trenches 27 to 34 inclusive.

CENTRE GROUP (b)

1st:, 2nd:, and 3rd: Staffs, and 1st: Lines: Battery under Command of Lieut: Colonel Sir H. Child will cover Trenches 35 to 40 inclusive.

The 4th: Belgian Battery will remain under the Command of O.C. RIGHT GROUP, and cover Trenches 33, and 34.

These two Trenches, and Right Battalion 137th: Infantry Brigade will be in direct communication with the Battery, and will call on it direct for fire.

CONTINUED. Page (2)

CENTRE GROUP

(b) Communications with it from 137th: Infantry Brigade Headquarters, will be obtained through O.C. Artillery CENTRE GROUP.

LEFT GROUP.

(c) 2nd: and 3rd: Lines:, and 4th: Staffs: Battery under Command of Major F. Campbell Johnson will cover Trenches 41 (a) to A.3 inclusive.

(d) Headquarters 3rd: North Midland Brigade R.F.A. will come under the Command of 3rd: Division from the 21st: instant, and will go to rest, 1st: North Midland Brigade. R.F.A. taking over their Headquarters.

(e) The 20th: Trench Howitzer Battery will revert to the 46th: Division, and the 40th: Trench Howitzer Battery will revert to the 3rd: Division, both on the night 25th:/26th: August.

Captain. R.A.
for Brigade Major.

H.Q. R.A. 46th: Divisional Artillery.

ISSUED AT p.m. COPY NO: BY D.R.

46th: Division
3rd: Divisional Artillery
Right Group
Centre Group
Left Group.
~~[illegible]~~
137th: Infantry Brigade.
138th: Infantry Brigade.
139th: Infantry Brigade.
4th: North Midland Brigade.
War Diary (2)

46th Division

7103

121
7051

War Diary.

7th Regiment Belgian Field Artillery

September

Vol VII

29/10/15

Instructions regarding War Diaries and Intelligence Summaries are contained in F. S. Regs., Part II. and the Staff Manual respectively. Title Pages will be prepared in manuscript.

WAR DIARY
or
~~INTELLIGENCE~~ SUMMARY
(Erase heading not required.)

Army Form C. 2118

(79)

Place	Date	Hour	Summary of Events and Information	Remarks and references to Appendices
	1.9.15.	4.10 am	1st Bty shelled Trench mortars as reprisal (73 H.E.)	
		4.30 am	5th Bty fired Test 27 Register (1 Shrap)	
		4.30 am	4th Bty shelled Trench 34 Register as reprisal (56 H.E.)	
		5. am	5th Bty " " 35 " as reprisal (7 H.E.)	
		5. am	5th Bty fired Test 34 register (1 Shrap)	
		7. am & 1.15 pm	5th Bty shelled communications (9 Shrap) ordered by CRA	
		10.50 am	1st Bty shelled working party in front of 31 (1 Shrap 5 H.E.)	
		1.5 pm	6th Bty fired Test 29 Register (1 Shrap)	
		1.40 pm	3rd Bty fired Test 28 Register (1 Shrap)	
		4 pm & 4.17 pm	5th Bty shelled Communications (6 Shrap)	
		5.28 pm	6th Bty fired Test 29 Register (1 Shrap)	
		5.35 pm	5th Bty fired Test 27 " (1 Shrap)	
		6.33 pm	6th Bty " " 30 " (1 Shrap)	
		8.55 pm	4th Bty shelled 34 register as reprisal (8 H.E.)	
		10.50 pm	3rd Bty fired Test 28 register (1 Shrap)	
	2.9.15	12.10 am	6th Bty " " 30 " (1 Shrap)	
	"	2.46 am	5th Bty " " 27 " (1 Shrap)	
		9.40 am	6th Bty " " 30 " (1 Shrap)	
		9.50 am	1st Bty " " 32 " (1 Shrap)	
		2.20 pm	3rd Bty " " 28 " (1 Shrap)	
		2.40 pm	6th Bty " " 29 " (1 Shrap)	
		3.50 pm	3rd Bty shelled " 28 " as reprisal (12 H.E.)	
		3.25 pm	B/81 shelled German works in front of 33 – 3 hits recorded – work demolished (10 H.E.)	
		5.12 pm	3rd Bty shelled 28 register as reprisal (11 H.E.)	
		5.20 pm	5th Bty shelled 27 " as reprisal (12 Shrap)	
		5.40 pm	3rd Bty fired Test 28 Register (1 Shrap)	
		9.01 pm	2nd Bty " " 26 " (1 Shrap)	
		9.48 pm	3rd Bty " " 28 " (1 Shrap)	CES

Instructions regarding War Diaries and Intelligence Summaries are contained in F. S. Regs., Part II. and the Staff Manual respectively. Title Pages will be prepared in manuscript.

WAR DIARY
or
~~INTELLIGENCE SUMMARY~~
(Erase heading not required.)

Army Form C. 2118

(80)

Place	Date	Hour	Summary of Events and Information	Remarks and references to Appendices
	2.9.15	10.25 pm	1st Bty fired Test on 31 Register (1 Shrap)	
		10.52 pm	6th Bty " " " 29 " (1 Shrap)	
	3.9.15	3.5 am	6th Bty " " " 30 " (1 Shrap)	
		3.40 am	5th Bty " " " 27 " (1 Shrap)	
		8.35 am	4th Bty Shelled working party 34 register (12 H.E. 6 Sh)	
		2.30 pm	4th Bty Shelled working party 34 register (10 H.E.)	
		2.35 pm	3rd Bty fired Test 28 register (1 Shrap)	
		6.32 pm	1st Bty " " 32 " (1 Shrap)	
		8.47 pm	1st Bty " " 31 " (1 Shrap)	
		10 pm	3rd Bty " " 28 " (1 Shrap)	
		10.30 pm	6th Bty " " 30 " (1 Shrap)	
		11.04 pm	5th Bty " " 27 " (1 Shrap)	
	4.9.15	9. am	4th Bty Shelled working party in front of 34 (4 H.E)	
		1.29 pm	1st Bty " 32 register as reprisal (23 H.E.)	
		2.14 pm	3rd Bty fired Test 28 register (1 Shrap)	
		2.18 pm	4th Bty Shelled m.g. loop-hole 34/33 register (26 H.E.)	
		3.15 pm	1st Bty " 32 register as reprisal (9 H.E.)	
		1.40 pm	B/81 Shelled Support Trenches opposite 32 as reprisal (10 H.E.)	
		5.57 pm	5th Bty fired Test 27 register (1 Shrap)	
	5.9.15	1.18 am	3rd Bty " " 28 " (1 Shrap)	
		3.30 am	1st Bty fired on Hollebeke from Dummy position (12 Shrap)	
		9. am	3rd Bty " Test 28 register (1 Shrap)	
		9.5 am	3rd Bty Shelled 28 register as reprisal (8 H.E.)	
		1.50 pm	6th Bty fired Test 30 register (1 Shrap)	
		2 pm	4th Bty Shelled M.G. between 33/34 (6 H.E.)	
		2.37 pm	4th Bty Shelled 33 register as reprisal (40 H.E.)	
		2.40 pm	1st Bty " 32 " " " (40 H.E.)	
		10.25 am	B/81 Shelled gun emplacement opposite 28 (11 H.E.) – The 11th Round of lyddite exploded in the bore, wrecking the howitzer completely and killing 2 men + wounding another.	GS.

Instructions regarding War Diaries and Intelligence Summaries are contained in F. S. Regs., Part II. and the Staff Manual respectively. Title Pages will be prepared in manuscript.

WAR DIARY
or
INTELLIGENCE SUMMARY
(Erase heading not required.)

Army Form C. 2118

(81)

Place	Date	Hour	Summary of Events and Information	Remarks and references to Appendices
		5.45pm	5th Bty. shelled ~~Bomb throwers in Trench 27 (2 Shrap.)~~	
	5.9.15	6.10pm	5th Bty fired Test 27 register (1 Shrap)	
		8.45pm	3rd Bty shelled 28 register as reprisal (8 H.E.)	
		8.50pm	6th Bty shelled Hollebeke Chateau from Dummy position (20 Shrap)	
		11.18pm	1st Bty fired Test on 32 register (1 Shrap)	
		10.33pm	6th Bty. fired Test 29 (1 Shrap.)	
	6.9.15	2.30am	5th Bty fired Test 27 (1 Shrap)	
		4.44am	6th Bty fired Test 29 (1 Shrap.)	C.S.
		12.30pm	4 Heavy Shell (possibly 21 cm.) fell between DICKEBUSCH Rd. + 3rd Bty. – killing 1 NCO in B/81.	
		12.33pm	6th Bty. fired Test 29 (1 Shrap.)	
		During morning	6th Bty. shelled ~~HOLLEB~~ CHATEAU O 4 d (37 Shrap) from false posn. –	
		1.16pm	5th Bty shelled Revolver gun at I 34. d 4 8 (24 HE) – the shoot being interrupted in the middle by the cutting of telephone line.	
		1.30pm	4 Heavy Shell again fell close to DICKEBUSCH Road – 2 of them in B/81s position –	
		1.35pm	4th Bty. shelled working party observed at I 34 d 8 8.	
			The shelling of DICKEBUSCH Road noted above was probably caused by numbers of wagons moving along the road from YPRES – (14 about) – ~~laden with bricks. etc.~~ –	C.B.
		3.57pm	3rd Bty fired Test 28 (1 Shrap.)	
		5.45pm	5th Bty fired Test 27 (1 Shrap.)	
		9.40pm	1st Bty fired Test 32 (1 Shrap.)	
		12.40am	1st Bty fired Test 32 (1 Shrap.)	
	7/9/15	2.22am	6th Bty fired Test 30 (1 Shrap.)	
		3.19am	5th Bty fired Test 27 (1 Shrap.)	
		4.30am	3rd Bty. fired Test 28 (1 Shrap.)	
		4.45am	3rd Bty ~~fired~~ shelled 28 Register at request of Trenches (4 Shrap.)	
		10am	1st Bty. shelled working party opp. 32 (5 Shrap.)	
		12.20am	3rd Bty. shelled German Battery firing from O 4 c 7 5 (40 HE 20 Shrap). This German Battery had been seen firing on 6th inst.	C.B.

Instructions regarding War Diaries and Intelligence Summaries are contained in F. S. Regs., Part II. and the Staff Manual respectively. Title Pages will be prepared in manuscript.

WAR DIARY
or
INTELLIGENCE SUMMARY
(Erase heading not required.)

Army Form C. 2118

(82)

Place	Date	Hour	Summary of Events and Information	Remarks and references to Appendices
7	7/9/15	1pm	B/81 shelled Same Btz (9 kz ddik)	
		1.35pm	4th Btz ~~shelled~~ fired Test 34 (1 Shrap.)	
		2.35pm	3rd Btz fired Test 28 (1 Shrap.)	C.S.
		2.50pm	1st Btz shelled Working party opposite 32. (8 Shrap.)	
		3. pm - 7pm	4th Btz advanced gun fired 11 Shr. from false posn. -	
		3.30pm	- - fired Test 34 (2S) 4.22pm 3rd Btz fired Test 28 (1S)	
		4.51pm	6th Btz - - 29 (1S)	
		5.52pm	5th Btz - - 27 (1S)	
		5.50pm	1st Btz shelled T. Ms. opp. 32 (45 HE) as Reprisals -	
		6.50pm	4th Btz - 34 Register (4 S) as Reprisals.	
		7.39pm	3rd Btz fired Test 28 (1S.)	
		7.40pm	3rd Btz advanced gun fired 28 Shr. from false posn. -	
		11.54pm	6th Btz fired Test 29 (1S.)	
	8/9/15	8.30am	5th Btz fired Test 27 (1S)	
		9.15am	3rd Btz fired Test 28 (1S)	
		10.25am	6th Btz fired 13 H.E. at house 0.4.b.5.8. - Registration -	
		2.25pm	4th Btz fired Test 34 (1S)	
		2.45pm	6th Btz fired Test 30 (1S)	C.S.
		4.13pm	1st Btz shelled 31 & 32 register at request of trenches (40 HE)	
		4.27pm	6th Btz shelled 29 & 30 register, as reprisal (40 H.E.)	
		4.30pm	1st Btz shelled 31 register at request of trenches. (29 HE)	
		5.15pm	4th Btz shelled 34 register on receipt of S.O.S. from trenches (71 Shrap)	
		5.32pm	4th Btz again shelled 34 register at request of trenches (12 H.E.)	
		5.35pm	1st Btz shelled 41 register as reprisal (13 HE)	
		5.41pm	4th Btz shelled 34 register as reprisal (12 Shrap)	
		5.45pm	1st Btz shelled Trench mortar opposite 31 (9 H.E.)	

Instructions regarding War Diaries and Intelligence Summaries are contained in F. S. Regs., Part II. and the Staff Manual respectively. Title Pages will be prepared in manuscript.

WAR DIARY
or
INTELLIGENCE SUMMARY
(Erase heading not required.)

Army Form C. 2118

83

Place	Date	Hour	Summary of Events and Information	Remarks and references to Appendices
	8/9	6.5pm	1st Bty shelled Trench Mortar opposite 31 (3 H.E.)	
		6.8pm	4th " " 34 register as reprisal (12 H.E.)	
		6.45pm	1st " fired Test 32 register (1 H.E.)	
		7.42pm	6th " " " 30 " (1 H.E.)	
		9.15pm	3rd " shelled German Transport heard in front of 28 (4 H.E.)	
		9.20pm	3rd " " " " " " " " (2 H.E.)	
		10.45pm	6th " fired Test 30 register (1 H.E.)	
	9/9	3.30pm	6th " shelled 30 register as reprisal (30 H.E.) ordered by Bm, 139th	
		4.24pm	3rd " fired Test 28 register (1 H.E.)	
		5.35pm	5th " " " 27 " (1 H.E.)	
		6.24pm	3rd " " " 28 " (1 H.E.)	
		11.25pm	1st " " " 32 " (1 H.E.)	
		3.32am	5th " " " 27 " (1 H.E.)	
		5.30am	4th " shelled 34 register as reprisal (12 H.E.)	
		5.45am	1st " " 32 " " " (6 H.E.)	
		5.45pm	5th " " Bty in 04C 7/3 as reprisal (25 H.E.)	
		11.45pm	3rd " fired Test 28 register (1 Sh)	
	10/9	12.23am	1st " " " 31 " (1 Sh)	
		3.47am	5th " " " 27 " (1 Sh)	
	9/9	4.15pm	B/51 shelled enemy's works in front of 27 - (34 H.E.) hits recorded.	
	10/9	11.4pm	3rd Bty fired Test 28 register (1 Sh)	
	11/9	12.25am	1st " " " 31 " (1 Sh)	
		2.20pm	3rd " " " 28 " (1 Sh)	
		6.7pm	5th " " " 27 " (1 H.E.)	
		6.25pm	1st " " " 31 " (1 H.E.)	

Army Form C. 2118

84

Instructions regarding War Diaries and Intelligence Summaries are contained in F. S. Regs., Part II. and the Staff Manual respectively. Title Pages will be prepared in manuscript.

WAR DIARY
or
~~INTELLIGENCE SUMMARY~~
(Erase heading not required.)

Place	Date	Hour	Summary of Events and Information	Remarks and references to Appendices
	11/9	9-9.30pm	3rd Bty shelled communications in front of Chateau O4d (30 H.E.) ordered by CRA	
		9.26pm	1st " fired Test 32 register (1 H.E)	
		9.37pm	6th " " " 29 " (1 H.E.)	
		10.41pm	3rd " " " 28 " (1 H.E)	
	12/9	4.25am	5th " " " 27 " (1 H.E)	
		7.33am	5th " Shelled 27 register as reprisal (12 H.E)	
		11.35am	3rd " fired Test 28 register (1 H.E)	
		12.05pm	6th " Shelled communications (1 H.E) in order to test buffer.	
		1.50pm	5th " " 27 register as reprisal (11 H.E)	
		11.50am	B/81 Shelled Hollebeke Chateau left lodge - Big explosion caused - 3 detonations close to out-house, amm. depot believed to have been blown up. (7 H.E)	
		4.38pm	5th Bty fired test 27 register (1 H.E)	
		5.50pm	6th " " " 32 " (1 H.E)	
		6.2pm	1st " " " 28 " (1 H.E)	
		8.45pm	3rd " " " 31 " (1 H.E)	
		10.40pm	1st " " " 30 " (1 H.E)	
		10.54pm	6th " " " 29 " (1 H.E)	
	13/9	2.45am	3rd " " " 28 " (1 H.E)	
		4.8am	5th " " " 27 " (1 H.E)	
		2.30pm	3rd " " " 28 " (1 H.E)	
		2.15pm	6th " " " 29 " (1 H.E)	
		6.30pm	4th " shelled armoured train on YPRES-COURTRAI line (8 H.E) Result satisfactory as train went away. The arrival & departure of this train can only be judged by sound.	
		7.00pm	5th Bty fired Test 27 register (1 H.E)	
		7.30pm	5th " Shelled 27 register as reprisal (4 H.E)	
		9.30pm	6th " fired Test 29 " (1 H.E.)	
		9.36pm	3rd " " " 28 " (1 H.E.)	
		10.15pm	1st " " " 31 " (1 H.E)	
	14/9	12.35am	5th " " " 27 " (1 H.E.)	
		8.45am	4th " Shelled 34 register (2nd line) working party (6 H.E)	

Instructions regarding War Diaries and Intelligence Summaries are contained in F. S. Regs., Part II. and the Staff Manual respectively. Title Pages will be prepared in manuscript.

WAR DIARY
or
~~INTELLIGENCE SUMMARY~~
(Erase heading not required.)

Army Form C. 2118

85

Place	Date	Hour	Summary of Events and Information	Remarks and references to Appendices
	14/9	11.am	3rd Bty shelled 27 register (fire & support) 50 HE. ordered by CRA	
		11.am	6th – – Trenches between O4a 2/4 & O4a 5/6 (50 HE) –"–	
		11.10am	4th – – 35 register as reprisal (28 HE)	
		11.15am	3rd – – Chateau MAHIEU & trenches in front (60 HE) –"–	
		11.15am	6th – – Same Targets as 3rd Bty (60 HE) –"–	
		11.35am	1st – – 31 register as reprisal (6 HE)	
		11.40am	1st – – – – (5 HE)	
		2.20pm	6th – fired Test 30 – (1 HE)	
		3.20pm	1st – Shelled working party 31 register (2nd line) (6 HE)	
		11.15am	B/81 shelled Chateau MAHIEU (30 HE) –"–	
		4.55pm	1st – fired Test 32 register (1 HE)	
		6.00pm	5th – – – 27 – (1 HE)	
		6.8pm	3rd – – – 28 – (2 HE)	
		8.25pm	1st – – – 31 – (1 HE)	
		10.20pm	6th – – – 30 – (1 HE)	
		10.27pm	6th – – – 30 – (1 HE)	
		11.16pm	3rd – – – 28 – (1 HE)	
	15/9	4.33am	5th – – – 27 – (1 HE)	
		9.53am	1st – Shelled working party 31 register (6 HE)	
		1.57pm	6th – fired Test 30 register (1 HE)	
		2.19pm	3rd – – – 28 – (1 HE)	
		2.40pm	4th – Shelled working party constructing dug-out at I34 d 9/8 (28 HE)	
		4.15pm	1st – fired Test 32 register (1 HE)	
		5.10pm	5th – – – 27 – (1 HE)	
		9.47pm	3rd – – – 28 – (1 HE)	
		10.17pm	1st – – – 31 – (1 HE)	
	16/9	2.35am	6th – – – 29 – (1 HE)	
		11.57am	3rd – – – 28 – (1 HE)	
		12.40pm	1st – Shelled – 32 – (6 HE)	
		3.2pm	5th – – works in front of 27 (22 HE) works destroyed	
		3.30pm	4th – – M.G. emplacement in front of 34 (22 HE) embrasure destroyed	

1875 Wt. W593/826 1,000,000 4/15 J.B.C. & A. A.D.S.S./Forms/C. 2118.

Instructions regarding War Diaries and Intelligence Summaries are contained in F. S. Regs., Part II. and the Staff Manual respectively. Title Pages will be prepared in manuscript.

WAR DIARY
or
~~INTELLIGENCE SUMMARY~~

(Erase heading not required.)

Army Form C. 2118

86

Place	Date	Hour	Summary of Events and Information	Remarks and references to Appendices
	16/9	5.5 pm	1st Bty Shelled 32 register as reprisal (12 HE)	
		5.10 "	4 " " MG emplacement 34 register (32 HE)	
		5.23 "	1st " " 32 register as reprisal (15 HE)	
		5.49 "	5 " fired Test 27 " (1 HE)	
		9.5 "	3 " " 28 " "	
	17/9	12.35 am	6 " " 30 " "	
		4.12 "	5 " " 27 " "	
		8.15 am	1 " " 32 "	
		2.35 pm	4th " Shelled M.G. emplacement 34 register (30 HE)	
		2.45 pm	B/81 Shelled dug-outs and O.P. in front of Chateau MAHIEU (20 HE) good effect.	
		4.35 pm	4th Bty " armoured train on YPRES-COURTRAI railway (8 HE)	
		5.2 pm	5th " fired Test 27 register (1 HE)	
		6.20 pm	3rd " " 28 "	
		6.30 pm	4th " Shelled points I35a 3/0 and I35a 6/5 (14 HE)	
		7.20 pm	1st " " 32 register as reprisal (3 HE)	
	18/9	1.8 am	6th " fired Test 29 register (1 HE)	
		1.40 am	1 " Shelled 31 register as reprisal (10 HE)	
		4.45 am	1 " " 31 " " (10 HE)	
		5 am	1 " " 31 " " (5 HE)	
		5.15 am	1 " " 31 " " (20 HE)	
		5.20 am	3rd " fired Test 28 " (1 HE)	
		5.55 am	4th " Shelled 34 register " (9 HE)	
		6 am	1st " " 31 " " (9 HE)	
		6.6 am	6th " " 30 " " (5 HE)	
		6.15 am	1st " " 31 " " (10 HE)	
		11.45 am	4th " Shelled working party in front of 33 (16 Sh)	
		12.59 pm	6th " fired Test 30 register (1 HE)	
		2.50 pm	1st " Shelled 31 " as reprisal (10 HE)	
		3.5 pm	1st " " Trench mortar in front of 31 (8 HE)	
		3.43 pm	1st " " " " (1 HE)	
		4.44 pm	6th " fired Test 29 register (1 HE)	
		7.18 pm	3rd " " " 28 " (1 HE)	

1875 Wt. W593/826 1,000,000 4/15 J.B.C. & A. A.D.S.S./Forms/C. 2118.

Instructions regarding War Diaries and Intelligence Summaries are contained in F. S. Regs., Part II. and the Staff Manual respectively. Title Pages will be prepared in manuscript.

WAR DIARY
or
INTELLIGENCE SUMMARY
(Erase heading not required.)

Army Form C. 2118

87

Place	Date	Hour	Summary of Events and Information	Remarks and references to Appendices
	19/9	7.25 pm	5th Bty fired Test 27 register (1 HE)	
		11.6 pm	6th – – – 29 – –	
	20/9	12.8 am	6th – – – – – –	
		1.52 am	6th – – – – – –	
		5.20 am	5th – – – 27 – –	
		7.20 am	3rd – – – 28 – –	
		9.51 am	1st – – – 32	
		9.45 am	4th – shelled working party in I24 d 4/5 (15 HE)	
		11.30 pm	B/81 shelled Off Lodge of Chateau MAHIEU – registration (11 HE)	
		2.35 pm	B/81 – House opposite 37 (I35 b 4/6) – registration (13 HE)	
		5.10 pm	5th – works – 27 (12 HE)	
		5.22 pm	3rd – fired Test 28 register (1 HE)	
		8.1 pm	5th – shelled 27 register as reprisal (1 HE)	
		9.51 pm	1st – fired Test 32 – (1 HE)	
		11.50 pm	3rd – – – 28 – –	
		11.52 pm	1st – – – 32 – –	
	21/9	12.40 pm	6th – – – 29 – –	
		5.20 am	5th – – – 27 – –	
		12.55 pm	1st – – – 32 – –	
		1. pm	6th – – – 29 – –	
		2.20 pm	4th – – – 34 – –	
	22/9	11.15 am	B/81 shelled Off Lodge Hollebeke Chateau registration (14 HE)	
		11.35 am	Hollebeke Chateau – (6 HE)	
		9. pm	3rd Bty fired Test 28 register (1 HE)	
	23/9	1. am	6th – – – 29 – (1 HE)	
		11.29 am	1st – – – 32 – (1 HE)	
		4 pm – 4.45 pm	4th Bty shelled 33 – fire + support trenches, very effective fire observed (40 HE)	
		4 pm – 4.45 pm	3rd – – house at O4 b 0/3 – large portion destroyed (40 HE)	
		4 pm – 4.45 pm	6th – – 30 register fire and support trenches – parapet badly damaged on front of 50 metres (40 HE)	
		4 pm – 4.45 pm	1st – – 31 and 32 register fire and support trenches – very good effect. (40 HE)	
		6.50 pm	6th Bty fired Test 29 register (1 HE)	

1875 Wt. W593/826 1,000,000 4/15 J.B.C. & A. A.D.S.S./Forms/C. 2118.

Instructions regarding War Diaries and Intelligence Summaries are contained in F. S. Regs., Part II. and the Staff Manual respectively. Title Pages will be prepared in manuscript.

WAR DIARY
or
~~INTELLIGENCE~~ SUMMARY
(Erase heading not required.)

Army Form C. 2118

88

Place	Date	Hour	Summary of Events and Information	Remarks and references to Appendices
	22/9	10 pm	3rd Bty fired Test 29 register (1 HE.)	
		10.40 pm	6th " " " 28 " "	
		11.10 pm	1st " " " 31 " "	
		12.5 pm	6th " shelled 30 register with very good effect (45 HE)	
		12.5 pm	3rd " " house 04 b o/3 – good effect but no direct hits obtained (45 HE)	
		12.5 pm	4th " " 33 register with good effect (45 HE)	
		12.5 pm	1st " " 31 + 32 register " " (45 HE)	
		1.45 pm	3rd " " 28 " as reprisal (10 HE)	
		2.47 pm	3rd " fired Test 28 " (1 HE)	
	24/9	2.35 am	1st " " " 31 "	
		4.20 am	1st " shelled support trenches 31 and 32 register (45 HE)	
		4.20 am	3rd " " house and dug-outs at 04 d o/3 (45 HE)	
		4.20 am	4th " " 33 register – fire & support (45 HE)	
		4.30 am	6th " " 30 " " " (45 HE)	
		10.50 am	6th " fired Test 30 " (1 HE)	
		1.3 pm	1st " shelled Trench 31 register as reprisal (7 HE)	
		1.10 pm	1st " " " " " " (3 HE)	
		1.16 pm	6th " " " 30 " " (18 HE)	
		2.43 pm	3rd " fired Test 28 " (1 HE)	
		1.15 pm	B/81 shelled Hill 60 for registration (4 HE)	
		2.15 pm	B/81 " House 04 b o/5 " (4 HE)	
		7.37 pm	3rd " fired Test 28 register (1 HE)	
		7.49 pm	3rd " " " 29 " (1 HE)	
		10.25 pm	3rd " " " 29 " (1 HE)	
	25/9	2.55 am	3rd " " " 28 " (1 HE)	
		3.50 am – 5.40 am	3rd Bty shelled O.Ps at 04 b o/3 (133 HE)	
		3.50 am – 4.20 am	1st " " C.T.s from I 34 d 4/4 to I 34 d 7/9 (60 HE) (60 Sh)	
		3.50 am – 4.20 am	6th " " " I 35 b 8/7 to I 35 c 10/5	
		3.55 am – 4.20 am	5th " " enemy's Bties in 04 d 4/4, 04 c 8/0, 05 b 2/6 (96 HE) (60 Sh)	
		4.58 am – 5.3 am	1st " " 31 and 32 register as reprisal (12 HE)	
		5.13 am	1st " " " " " " (12 HE)	
		5.40 am	6th " " 35 register " (6 HE)	

Instructions regarding War Diaries and Intelligence Summaries are contained in F. S. Regs., Part II. and the Staff Manual respectively. Title Pages will be prepared in manuscript.

WAR DIARY
or
~~INTELLIGENCE SUMMARY~~
(Erase heading not required.)

Army Form C. 2118

89

Place	Date	Hour	Summary of Events and Information	Remarks and references to Appendices
	25/9	6.7am	6th Bty shelled trench mortar in 2nd line trench opposite 30 (16 HE)	
		6.15am	4th " " 34 register as reprisal (6 HE)	
		6.15am	1st " " 32 " " " (30 HE, 20 Sh)	
		6.20am	4th " " 33+34 " " " (40 HE)	
		6.35am	6th " " Wall hiding M.G. 30 register (14 HE)	
		6.35am	1st " " 32 register as reprisal (10 HE)	
		9.26am	3rd " " O.Ps at 04 b 0/3 (28 HE)	
		9.28am	2nd " " Bty at 04 C 8/0 as reprisal (40 HE 20 Sh)	
		9.55am	3rd " " " " 04 d 4/4 " " (40 HE 20 Sh)	
		9.55am	5th " " " " 04 d 4/4 " " (10 HE)	
		10.4am	2nd " " " " 04 C 7/5 " " (50 HE 10 Sh)	
		10.5am	6th " " Trench mortar 2nd line trench opposite 30 (20 HE)	
		10.5am	5th " " Bty at 04 C 8/0 as reprisal (10 HE)	
		10.10am	4th " " " at I 35 d 7/9 " " (40 HE 20 Sh)	
		10.14am	5th " " " " 05 b 2/6 " " (10 HE)	
		10.17am	3rd " " " " 04 b 9/9 " " (40 HE 20 Sh)	
		10.20am	6th " " " " 05 b 2/6 " " (40 HE 20 Sh)	
		10.34am	3rd " " O Ps at 04 b 0/3 (52 HE)	
		11.10am	2nd " " O Ps at 04 b 0/3 (66 HE)	
		3.35pm	2nd " " O Ps at 04 b 0/3 (31 HE)	
		3.40pm	5th " " Bty 05 b 2/6 as reprisal (30 HE)	
		4.32pm	5th " " " 01 0 b 5/6 " (40 HE 10 Sh)	
		7.10pm	6th " " " 05 b 2/6 " (20 HE 10 Sh)	
		7.14pm	4th " " " I 35 d 7/9 " (20 HE 10 Sh)	
		7.44pm	3rd " fired Test 28 register (1 HE)	
	26/9	3.50pm	2nd " " " 28 " (1 HE)	
		4.8pm	6th " " " 30 " (1 HE)	
		4.37pm	1st " " " 32 " (1 HE)	
		4.45pm	6th " " " 29 " (1 HE)	
		8.47pm	1st " shelled 32 " as reprisal (2 HE)	
		11.46pm	5th " fired Test 27 " (1 HE)	
	27/9	2.30pm	3rd " " " 28 " (1 HE)	
		3.27pm	1st " " " 32 " (1 HE)	
		2.41pm	5th " " " 27 " (1 HE)	
		3.44pm	6th " " " 30 " (1 HE)	

1875 Wt. W593/826 1,000,000 4/15 J.B.C. & A. A.D.S.S./Forms/C. 2118.

Army Form C. 2118

90

Instructions regarding War Diaries and Intelligence Summaries are contained in F. S. Regs., Part II. and the Staff Manual respectively. Title Pages will be prepared in manuscript.

WAR DIARY
or
~~INTELLIGENCE~~ SUMMARY
(Erase heading not required.)

Place	Date	Hour	Summary of Events and Information	Remarks and references to Appendices
	27/9	4.8 pm	6th Bty fired Test 29 register to dug buffer (1 HE)	
		4.30 pm	5th ″ ″ ″ 27 ″ (1 HE)	
		9.16 pm	1st ″ ″ ″ 20 ″ (1 HE)	
		9.43 pm	3rd ″ ″ ″ 28 ″ (1 HE)	
	28/9	4.30 am	5th ″ ″ ″ 27 ″ (1 HE)	
		11.26 am	6th ″ ″ ″ 29 ″ (1 HE)	
		12.45 pm	5th ″ ″ ″ 27 ″ (1 HE)	
		12.48 pm	5th ″ shelled ″ ″ as reprisal (3 HE)	
		2.8 pm	5th ″ ″ ″ ″ (3 HE)	
		2.15 pm	4th ″ ″ 35 ″ – left of 2nd line as reprisal (10 HE)	
		3.3 pm	1st ″ fired Test 32 ″ (1 HE)	
		5.25 pm	5th ″ shelled enemy Transport at O4 d 4/4 (8 HE)	
		6.30 pm	1st ″ ″ Trench Mortar 31 register as reprisal (8 HE)	
		12 midnight	1st ″ fired Test 31 register (1 HE)	
	29/9	12.10 am	5th ″ ″ ″ 27 ″ (1 HE)	
		3.35 am	6th ″ ″ ″ 29 ″ (1 HE)	
		8.46 am	5th ″ ″ on Trench 27 ″ as reprisal (4 HE)	
		8.30 am	5th ″ ″ ″ 27 ″ ″ ″ (9 HE)	
		11.45 am	6th ″ ″ Test 29 ″ (1 HE)	
		12.15 pm	4th ″ ″ at Trench 35 ″ ″ ″ (20 HE)	
		5 pm	1st ″ ″ shelled armoured Train (4 HE)	
		5.32 pm	5th ″ ″ Test 27 register (1 HE)	
		5.42 pm	1st ″ ″ ″ 32 ″ (1 HE)	
		6.14 pm	3rd ″ ″ ″ 28 ″ (1 HE)	
	30/9	8.9 am	3rd ″ shelled 28 ″ as reprisal (6 HE)	
		8.30 am	4th ″ ″ 35 register (2nd line) as reprisal (8 HE)	
		1.20 pm	5th ″ ″ Bty at O 5 b 2/7 – CRA's order (24 HE)	
		2.40 pm	3rd ″ ″ Trench 28 register as reprisal (6 HE)	
		3 pm	5th ″ ″ Bty at O5 b 2/7 CRA's orders (40 HE)	
		3.40 pm	5th ″ ″ 27 register as reprisal (9 HE)	
		4.51 pm	5th ″ ″ 27 ″ ″ ″ (4 HE)	

1875 Wt. W593/826 1,000,000 4/15 J.B.C. & A. A.D.S.S./Forms/C. 2118.

Instructions regarding War Diaries and Intelligence Summaries are contained in F. S. Regs., Part II. and the Staff Manual respectively. Title Pages will be prepared in manuscript.

WAR DIARY
or
~~INTELLIGENCE SUMMARY~~
(Erase heading not required.)

Army Form C. 2118

91

Place	Date	Hour	Summary of Events and Information	Remarks and references to Appendices
	30/9	6.14 pm	5th Bty shelled 27 register as reprisal (16 HE)	
		6.25 pm	4 " " 33.34.35 " " " (112 HE 102 Sh)	
		6.30 pm	1 " " 30.31.32 " " " (180 HE)	
		6.30 pm	3 " " 28.29 " " " (74 HE)	
		6.35 pm	6 " " 29 " " " (51 HE)	
		6.42 pm	5 " " 27 " " " (16 HE)	
		7.20 pm	3 " " 28 " " " (18 HE)	
		8.55 pm	1 " " Trench Mortar " " (5 HE)	
		7.0 pm	B/81 " 28.29 " " (23 HE) at request from 139th Bde. (Inf.)	
			Losses during month.	
			Killed.	
	25/9.		3rd Bty - 1 Gr	
	30/9		6th " - 1 Trumpeter	
	30/9		6th " - 1 Gr	
			Wounded	
	15/9		1st " - 1 Gr	
	6/9		2nd " - 1 Gr	
	25/9		3rd " - 1 Gr	
	30/9		6th " - 1 Bombardier	
	30/9		6th " - 1 Gr (died of wounds on same day in Infirmary Poperinghe)	

7th Regiment Belgian Field Artillery.

1875 Wt. W593/826 1,000,000 4/15 J.B.C. & A. A.D.S.S./Forms/C. 2118.

Instructions regarding War Diaries and Intelligence Summaries are contained in F. S. Regs., Part II. and the Staff Manual respectively. Title Pages will be prepared in manuscript.

WAR DIARY
or
~~INTELLIGENCE SUMMARY~~
(Erase heading not required.)

Army Form C. 2118

(79)

Place	Date	Hour	Summary of Events and Information	Remarks and references to Appendices
	1.9.15	[illegible] am	1st Bty shelled Trench mortar as reprisal (73 H.E.)	
		[illegible] am	5th Bty fired Test 27 Register (1 shrap)	
		4.[illegible] am	6th Bty shelled Trench 34 Register as reprisal (56 H.E.)	
		5 am	5th Bty " " 35 " as reprisal (1 H.E.)	
		5. am	5th Bty fired Test 34 register (1 shrap)	
		7 am to 1.15 pm	5th Bty shelled communication (9 shrap) ordered by CRA	
		10.50 am	1st Bty shelled working party in front of 31 (1 shrap 5 H.E.)	
		1.5 pm	6th Bty fired Test 30 Register (1 shrap)	
		1.[illegible] pm	3rd Bty fired Test 28 Register (1 shrap)	
		4 pm to 4.17 pm	5th Bty shelled communication (6 shrap)	
		5.28 pm	6th Bty fired Test 29 Register (1 shrap)	
		5.[illegible] pm	5th Bty fired Test 27 " (1 shrap)	
		6.33 pm	6th Bty " " 30 " (1 shrap)	
		8.05 pm	4th Bty shelled 30 register as reprisal (5 H.E.)	
		10.50 pm	3rd Bty fired Test 28 register (1 shrap)	
	2.9.15	12.[illegible] am	6th Bty " " 30 " (1 shrap)	
		2.46 am	5th Bty " " 27 " (1 shrap)	
		9.40 am	6th Bty " " 30 " (1 shrap)	
		9.50 am	1st Bty " " 32 " (1 shrap)	
		2.20 pm	3rd Bty " " 28 " (1 shrap)	
		2.4[illegible] pm	6th Bty " " 29 " (1 shrap)	
		3.50 pm	3rd Bty shelled " 28 " as reprisal (12 H.E.)	
		3.25 pm	B/81 shelled German works in front of 33 – 3 hits recorded – work demolished (10 H.E.)	
		5.12 pm	3rd Bty shelled 28 register as reprisal (11 H.E.)	
		5.20 pm	5th Bty shelled 27 " as reprisal (12 shrap)	
		5.40 pm	3rd Bty fired Test 28 register (1 shrap)	
		9.01 pm	2nd Bty " " 26 " (1 shrap)	
		9.48 pm	3rd Bty " " 28 " (1 shrap)	CWS.

Instructions regarding War Diaries and Intelligence Summaries are contained in F. S. Regs., Part II. and the Staff Manual respectively. Title Pages will be prepared in manuscript.

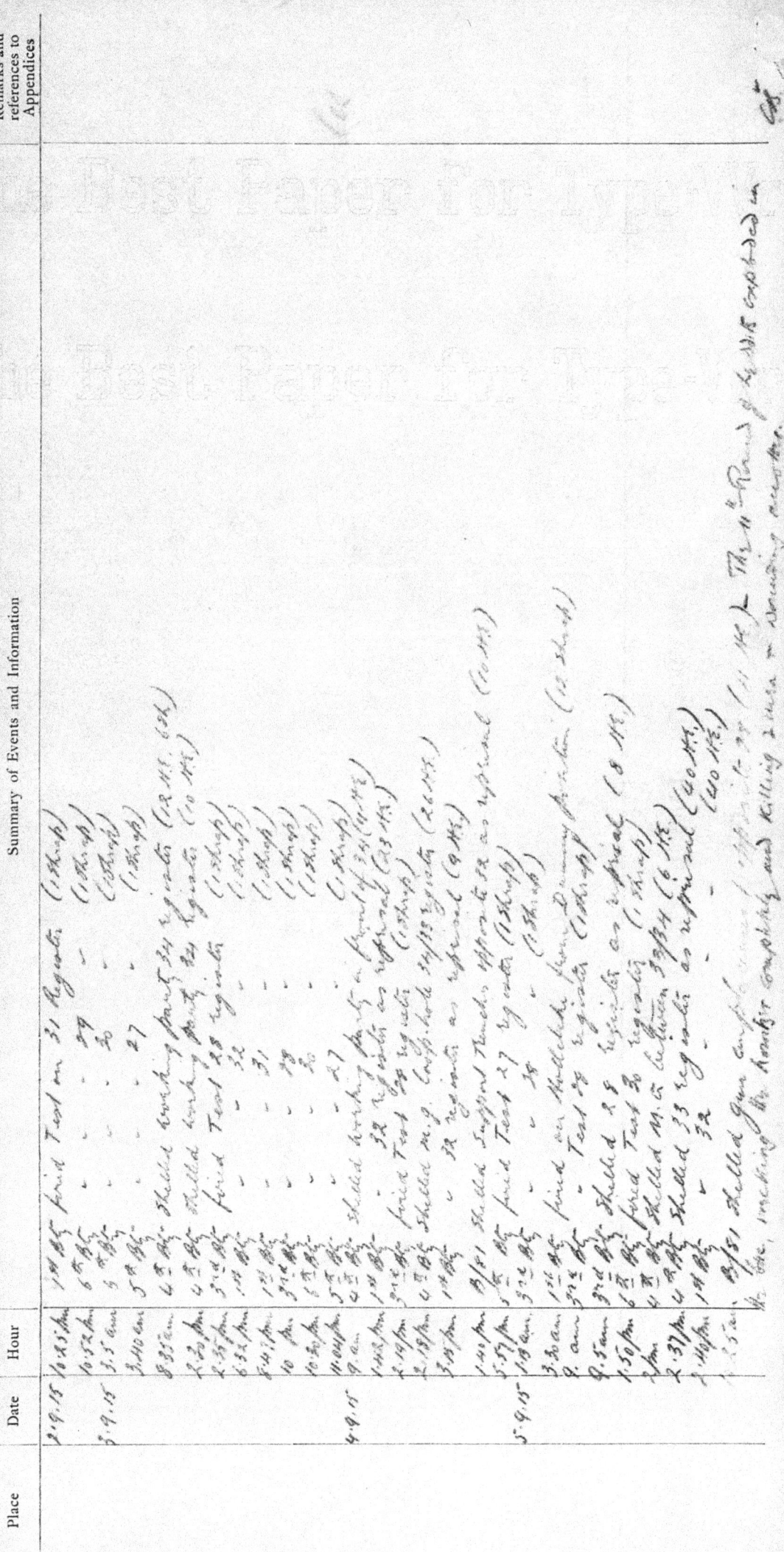

WAR DIARY
or
~~INTELLIGENCE SUMMARY~~
(Erase heading not required.)

Army Form C. 2118

(80)

Place	Date	Hour	Summary of Events and Information	Remarks and references to Appendices
	2.9.15	10.25 pm	1st Bty fired Test on 31 Register (1 Shrap)	
		10.52 pm	6th Bty " " " 29 " (1 Shrap)	
	3.9.15	3.5 am	6th Bty " " " 30 " (1 Shrap)	
		3.40 am	5th Bty " " " 27 " (1 Shrap)	
		8.35 am	4th Bty Shelled working party 34 register (12 H.E. 6 Sh)	
		2.20 pm	4th Bty Shelled working party 34 register (10 H.E.)	
		2.35 pm	3rd Bty fired Test 28 register (1 Shrap)	
		6.32 pm	1st Bty " " 32 " (1 Shrap)	
		8.47 pm	1st Bty " " 31 " (1 Shrap)	
		10 pm	3rd Bty " " 28 " (1 Shrap)	
		10.30 pm	6th Bty " " 30 " (1 Shrap)	
		11.04 pm	5th Bty " " 27 " (1 Shrap)	
	4.9.15	9. am	4th Bty Shelled working party in front of 34 (4 H.E.)	
		1.42 pm	1st Bty " 32 register as reprisal (23 H.E.)	
		2.14 pm	3rd Bty fired Test 28 register (1 Shrap)	
		2.18 pm	4th Bty Shelled M.G. loop-hole 34/33 register (26 H.E.)	
		3.15 pm	1st Bty " 32 register as reprisal (9 H.E.)	
		1.40 pm	B/81 Shelled Support Trenches opposite 32 as reprisal (10 H.E.)	
		5.57 pm	5th Bty fired Test 27 register (1 Shrap)	
	5.9.15	1.13 am	3rd Bty " " 28 " (1 Shrap)	
		3.30 am	1st Bty fired on Hollebeke from Dummy position (12 Shrap)	
		9. am	3rd Bty " Test 28 register (1 Shrap)	
		9.5 am	3rd Bty Shelled 28 register as reprisal (8 H.E.)	
		1.50 pm	6th Bty fired Test 30 register (1 Shrap)	
		2 pm	4th Bty Shelled M.G. between 33/34 (6 H.E.)	
		2.37 pm	4th Bty Shelled 33 register as reprisal (40 H.E.)	
		2.40 pm	1st Bty " 32 " " (40 H.E.)	
		1.25 am	B/81 Shelled gun emplacement opposite 28 (11 H.E.) — The 11th Round of the HE exploded in the bore, wrecking the howitzer completely and killing 2 men & wounding another.	

CS

Instructions regarding War Diaries and Intelligence Summaries are contained in F. S. Regs., Part II. and the Staff Manual respectively. Title Pages will be prepared in manuscript.

WAR DIARY
or
INTELLIGENCE SUMMARY
(Erase heading not required.)

Army Form C. 2118

(81)

Place	Date	Hour	Summary of Events and Information	Remarks and references to Appendices
		~~5.45pm~~	~~5th Bty shelled Bombthrowers in Trench 27 (3 shrap.)~~	
	5.9.15	6.10pm	5th Bty fired Test 27 register (1 shrap)	
		8.45pm	3rd Bty shelled 28 register as reprisal (8 H.E.)	
		8.50pm	6th Bty shelled Hollebeke Chateau from Dummy position (20 shrap)	
		11.18pm	1st Bty fired Test on 32 register (1 shrap)	
		10.32pm	6th Bty fired Test 29 (1 shrap.)	
	6.9.15	2.30am	5th Bty fired Test 27 (1 shrap)	C.B.
		4.44am	6th Bty fired Test 29 (1 shrap.)	
		12.30pm	4 Heavy Shell (possibly 21 cm.) fell between DICKEBUSCH Rd. + 3rd Bty. – killing 1 H.D. in B/81.	
		12.33pm	6th Bty fired Test 29 (1 shrap.)	
		During morning	6th Bty shelled ~~[illegible]~~ CHATEAU 04 d (8 shrap) from false posn.	
		1.16pm	5th Bty shelled Revolver gun at I 34. d 48 (24 HE) – the shoot being interrupted in the middle by the cutting of telephone line.	
		1.30pm	4 Heavy Shell again fell close to DICKEBUSCH Road – 2 of them in B/81 position.	
		1.35pm	4th Bty shelled Working party observed at I 34 d 5.8.	
			The shelling of DICKEBUSCH Road today & yesterday probably caused by movement of [illegible] along the road from YPRES – (14 wheel) – [illegible]	C.B.
		3.57pm	3rd Bty fired Test 28 (1 shrap)	
		5.45pm	5th Bty fired Test 27 (1 shrap.)	
		9.40pm	1st Bty fired Test 32 (1 shrap)	
	7/9/15	12.40am	1st Bty fired Test 32 (1 shrap)	
		2.32am	6th Bty fired Test 30 (1 shrap)	
		3.19am	5th Bty fired Test 27 (1 shrap)	
		4.30am	3rd Bty fired Test 28 (1 shrap)	
		4.45am	3rd Bty ~~fired~~ shelled 28 Register [illegible] (4 shrap)	
		10am	[illegible] Bty shelled Working party opp. 32 (5 shrap)	
		12.20pm	1st Bty shelled German Battery firing from O 4 c 75. (40 HE 20 Shrap). This German Battery had been seen firing on 6th [illegible]	C.B.

Instructions regarding War Diaries and Intelligence Summaries are contained in F. S. Regs., Part II. and the Staff Manual respectively. Title Pages will be prepared in manuscript.

WAR DIARY
or
INTELLIGENCE SUMMARY
(Erase heading not required.)

Army Form C. 2118

(82)

Place	Date	Hour	Summary of Events and Information	Remarks and references to Appendices
7	7/9/15	1pm	B/81 shelled Same Bty. (9 Hy [illegible])	
		1.35pm	4th Bty ~~shelled~~ fired Tект 34 (12 shrap.)	
		2.35pm	3rd Bty fired Tест 28 (15 shrap.)	
		2.50pm	1st Bty shelled working party opposite 32. (8 shrap.)	[initials]
		[illegible] 7pm	4th Bty advanced gun fired 11 Rds from false posn.	
		3.30pm	" " fired Tест 34 (25). 4.22pm 3rd Bty fired Tест 28 (15)	
		4.51pm	6th Bty " " 29 (15)	
		5.[illegible]pm	5th Bty " " 27 (15)	
		[illegible]pm	1st Bty shelled T. Rd. opp. 22 (40 HE) in Reprisals	
		6.50pm	4th Bty " 3 Registers (4 S) in Reprisals.	
		7.29pm	3rd Bty fired Tест 28 (15)	
		[illegible]pm	3rd Bty advanced gun fired 23 Rds from false posn.	
		[illegible]pm	6th Bty fired Tест 29 (15)	
	8/9/15	8.[illegible]am	5th Bty fired Tест 27 (15)	
		9.15am	3rd Bty fired Tест 28 (15)	
		[illegible]am	6th Bty fired 13 H.E. at [illegible] Registration	
		[illegible]pm	4th Bty fired Tест 34 (15)	
		[illegible]pm	6th Bty fired Tест [illegible] (12)	
		4.13pm	1st Bty shelled 31 + 32 registers at request of trenches (4 HE)	[initials]
		4.27pm	6th Bty shelled 29 + [illegible] [illegible] (14 HE)	
		4.[illegible]pm	1st Bty shelled 31 registers at request of trenches (20 HE)	
		5.15pm	4th Bty shelled 34 registers on receipt of [illegible] from trenches (71 shrap)	
		5.[illegible]pm	4th Bty [illegible] gun shelled 34 registers at request of trenches (12 HE)	
		5.[illegible]pm	1st Bty shelled 41 registers [illegible]	
		5.[illegible]pm	4th Bty shelled 34 registers [illegible] (12 shrap)	
		[illegible]pm	1st Bty shelled Trench mortar opposite 31 (9 HE)	

Instructions regarding War Diaries and Intelligence Summaries are contained in F. S. Regs., Part II. and the Staff Manual respectively. Title Pages will be prepared in manuscript.

WAR DIARY
or
INTELLIGENCE SUMMARY
(Erase heading not required.)

Army Form C. 2118

83

Place	Date	Hour	Summary of Events and Information	Remarks and references to Appendices
	8/9	6.5 pm	1st Bty shelled Trench Mortar opposite 31 (3 H.E.)	
		6.8 pm	6th " " 34 register as reprisal (12 H.E.)	
		6.45 pm	1st " fired Test 32 register (1 H.E.)	
		7.42 pm	6th " " " 30 " (1 H.E.)	
		9.15 pm	5th " shelled German Transport heard in front of 28 (4 H.E.)	
		9.20 pm	3rd " " " " " " " (2 H.E.)	
		10.15 pm	6th " fired Test 30 register (1 H.E.)	
	9/9	3.30 pm	6th " shelled 30 register as reprisal (30 H.E.) ordered by Bde. 139th	
		4.24 pm	3rd " fired Test 28 register (1 H.E.)	
		5.35 pm	5th " " " 27 " (1 H.E.)	
		6.24 pm	3rd " " " 28 " (1 H.E.)	
		11.25 pm	1st " " " 32 " (1 H.E.)	
		3.32 am	5th " " " 27 " (1 H.E.)	
		5.30 am	6th " shelled 34 register as reprisal (12 H.E.)	
		5.45 am 5.45 pm	5th " " Bty 32 in O4C 7/3 as reprisal (6 H.E.) (25 H.E.)	
		11.45 pm	3rd " fired Test 28 register (1 Sh)	
	10/9	12.23 am	1st " " " 31 " (1 Sh)	
		3.47 am	5th " " " 27 " (1 Sh)	
	9/9	4.15 pm	B/81 shelled enemy's works in front of 27 - (34 H.E.) hit recorded.	
	10/9	11.4 pm	3rd Bty fired Test 28 register (1 Sh)	
	11/9	12.25 am	1st " " " 31 " (1 Sh)	
		2.20 pm	3rd " " " 28 " (1 Sh)	
		6.7 pm	5th " " " 27 " (1 H.E.)	
		6.25 pm	1st " " " 31 " (1 H.E.)	

Instructions regarding War Diaries and Intelligence Summaries are contained in F. S. Regs., Part II. and the Staff Manual respectively. Title Pages will be prepared in manuscript.

WAR DIARY
or
~~INTELLIGENCE SUMMARY~~
(Erase heading not required.)

Army Form C. 2118

84

Date	Hour	Summary of Events and Information	Remarks and references to Appendices
11/9	9-9.30pm	3rd Bty shelled communications in front of Chateau O.4.d (20 HE) ordered by CRA	
	9.36pm	1st ″ fired Test 32 register (1 HE)	
	9.37pm	6th ″ ″ ″ 29 ″ (1 HE)	
	10.41pm	3rd ″ ″ ″ 28 ″ (1 HE)	
12/9	4.25am	5th ″ ″ ″ 27 (1 HE)	
	4.33am	5th ″ Shelled 27 register as reprisal (12 HE)	
	11.35am	3rd ″ fired Test 28 register (1 HE)	
	12.05pm	6th ″ Shelled communications (1 HE) in order to test buffer.	
	1.50pm	5th ″ ″ 27 register as reprisal (11 HE)	
	11.50am	8/81 Shelled Hollebeke Chateau left lodge - Big explosion caused - 3 detonations close to out-house, Ammn depot believed to have been blown up (7 HE)	
	4.38pm	5th Bty fired test 27 register (1 HE)	
	5.50pm	6th ″ ″ ″ 32 ″ (1 HE)	
	6.2pm	1st ″ ″ ″ 28 ″ (1 HE)	
	8.45pm	3rd ″ ″ ″ 31 ″ (1 HE)	
	10.40pm	1st ″ ″ ″ 30 ″ (1 HE)	
	10.54pm	6th ″ ″ ″ 29 ″ (1 HE)	
13/9	2.45am	3rd ″ ″ ″ 28 ″ (1 HE)	
	4.8am	5th ″ ″ ″ 27 ″ (1 HE)	
	2.30pm	3rd ″ ″ ″ 28 ″ (1 HE)	
	2.45pm	6th ″ ″ ″ 29 ″ (1 HE)	
	6.30pm	4th ″ shelled armoured train on YPRES-COURTRAI line (8 HE) Result satisfactory as train went away. The arrival & departure of this train can only be judged by sound.	
	7.00pm	5th Bty fired Test 27 register (1 HE)	
	7.30pm	5th ″ Shelled 27 register as reprisal (4 HE)	
	9.30pm	6th ″ fired Test 29 ″ (1 HE)	
	9.36pm	3rd ″ ″ ″ 28 ″ (1 HE)	
	10.15pm	1st ″ ″ ″ 31 ″ (1 HE)	
14/9	4.32am	5th ″ ″ ″ 27 ″ (1 HE)	
	8.45am	4th ″ Shelled 34 register (2nd line) working party (6 HE)	

1875 Wt. W593/826 1,000,000 4/15 J.B.C. & A. A.D.S.S./Forms/C. 2118.

Instructions regarding War Diaries and Intelligence Summaries are contained in F. S. Regs., Part II. and the Staff Manual respectively. Title Pages will be prepared in manuscript.

WAR DIARY
or
~~INTELLIGENCE SUMMARY.~~
(Erase heading not required.)

Army Form C. 2118

85

Place	Date	Hour	Summary of Events and Information	Remarks and references to Appendices
	14/9	11 am	3rd Bty shelled 27 registr (fire the support) 50 HE, ordered by CRA	
		11 am	6th " — Trenches between 04a 2/4 & 04a 5/6 (50 HE) — " —	
		11.10 am	4th " — 35 registr as reprisal (23 HE)	
		11.15 am	3rd " — Chateau MAHIEU & trenches in front (60 HE) — " —	
		11.30 am	6th " — Same Targets as 3rd Bty (60 HE) — " —	
		11.35 am	1st " — 31 registr as reprisal (6 HE)	
		11.40 am	1st " — — " — (5 HE)	
		2.20 pm	6th " fired Test 30 — (1 HE)	
		3.00 pm	1st " Shelled working party 31 registr (2nd line) (6 HE)	
		4.15 am	[illegible] shelled Chateau MAHIEU (30 HE) — " —	
		4.55 pm	1st " fired Test 32 register (1 HE)	
		6.00 pm	5th " — " — 27 — (1 HE)	
		6.8 pm	3rd " — " — 28 — (1 HE)	
		8.25 pm	1st " — " — 31 — (1 HE)	
		10.25 pm	6th " — " — 30 — (1 HE)	
		10.27 pm	6th " — " — 30 — (1 HE)	
		11.10 pm	3rd " — " — 28 — (1 HE)	
	15/9	9.33 am	5th " — " — 27 — (1 HE)	
		9.53 am	1st " Shelled working party 31 register (6 HE)	
		1.57 pm	6th " fired Test 30 register (1 HE)	
		2.19 pm	3rd " — " — 28 — (1 HE)	
		2.40 pm	4th " Shelled working party constructing dug-out at I 34 d 9/5 (25 HE)	
		4.15 pm	1st " fired Test 32 register (1 HE)	
		5.10 pm	5th " — " — 27 — (1 HE)	
		9.47 pm	3rd " — " — 28 — (1 HE)	
		10.17 pm	1st " — " — 31 — (1 HE)	
	16/9	2.33 am	6th " — " — 29 — (1 HE)	
		11.57 am	3rd " — " — 28 — (1 HE)	
		12.11 pm	1st " shelled 32 — (6 HE)	
		2.2 pm	[illegible] " works in front of 27 (22 HE) [illegible] destroyed	
		3.3 pm	4th " M.G. emplacement in front of 34 (22 HE) embrasure destroyed	

1875 Wt. W593/826 1,000,000 4/15 J.B.C. & A. A.D.S.S./Forms/C. 2118.

Instructions regarding War Diaries and Intelligence Summaries are contained in F. S. Regs., Part II. and the Staff Manual respectively. Title Pages will be prepared in manuscript.

WAR DIARY
or
~~INTELLIGENCE SUMMARY~~
(Erase heading not required.)

Army Form C. 2118

86

Place	Date	Hour	Summary of Events and Information	Remarks and references to Appendices
	16/9	5.5pm	1st Bty Shelled 32 registr as reprisal (12 HE)	
		5.10 "	4 " " MG emplacement 34 registr (32 HE)	
		5.23 "	1st " " 32 registr as reprisal (15 HE)	
		5.49 "	5 " fired Test 27 " (1 HE)	
		9.3 "	3 " " 28 " "	
	17/9	12.35am	6 " " 30 " "	
		4.12 "	5 " " 27 " "	
		8.15am	1 " " 32 " "	
		2.35pm	4th " Shelled M.G. emplacement 34 registr (30 HE)	
		2.45pm	B/81 Shelled dug-outs and O.P. in front of Chateau MAHIEU (20 HE) good effect.	
		4.35pm	Nth Bty " armoured train on YPRES-COURTRAI railway (8 HE)	
		5.2pm	5th " fired Test 27 registr (1 HE)	
		6.30pm	3rd " " 28 "	
		6.3pm	4th " Shelled points I35a 9/0 and I35a 6/5 (14 HE)	
		7.30pm	1st " " 32 registr as reprisal (8 HE)	
	18/9	1.8am	6th " fired Test 29 registr (1 HE)	
		1.45am	1st " Shelled 31 registr as reprisal (10 HE)	
		4.45am	1 " " 31 " " (10 HE)	
		5 am	1 " " 31 " " (5 HE)	
		5.15am	1 " " 31 " " (20 HE)	
		5.30am	3rd " fired Test 28 " (1 HE)	
		5.35am	4th " Shelled 34 registr " (9 HE)	
		6 am	1st " " 31 " " (9 HE)	
		6.1 am	6th " " 30 " " (5 HE)	
		6.15am	1st " " 31 " " (10 HE)	
		11.45am	4th " Shelled working party in front of 33 (16 Sh)	
		12.59pm	6th " fired Test 30 registr . (1 HE)	
		2.52pm	1st " Shelled 31 " as reprisal (10 HE)	
		3.5pm	1st " " Trench mortar in front of 31 (8 HE)	
		3.43pm	1st " " " " (1 HE)	
		4.44pm	6th " fired Test 29 registr (1 HE)	
		7.18pm	3rd " " 28 " (1 HE)	

1875 Wt. W593/826 1,000,000 4/15 J.B.C. & A. A.D.S.S./Forms/C. 2118.

Instructions regarding War Diaries and Intelligence Summaries are contained in F. S. Regs., Part II. and the Staff Manual respectively. Title Pages will be prepared in manuscript.

WAR DIARY
or
INTELLIGENCE SUMMARY
(Erase heading not required.)

Army Form C. 2118

87

Place	Date	Hour	Summary of Events and Information	Remarks and references to Appendices
	19/9	7.25 pm	5th Bty fired Test 27 register (1 HE)	
		10.6 pm	6th – – – 29 – –	
	20/9	12.8 am	6th – – – – – –	
		1.52 am	6th – – – – – –	
		5.20 am	5th – – – 27 – –	
		7.34 am	3rd – – – 28 – –	
		9.57 am	1st – – – 32 – –	
		9.45 am	4th – shelled working party in I24 d 4/5 (15 HE)	
		4.3 pm	B/81 shelled left Lodge of Chateau MAHIEU – registration (11 HE)	
		2.55 pm	B/81 – – house opposite 57 (I35 b 4/6) – registration (13 HE)	
		5.10 pm	5th – – works – 27 (12 HE)	
		5.22 pm	3rd – fired Test 28 register (1 HE)	
		8.1 pm	5th – shelled 27 register as reprisal (1 HE)	
		9.51 pm	1st – fired Test 32 – (1 HE)	
		10.52 pm	3rd – – – 28 – –	
		11.52 pm	1st – – – 32 – –	
	21/9	12.40 am	6th – – – 29 – –	
		5.20 am	5th – – – 27 – –	
		12.55 pm	1st – – – 32 – –	
		1. pm	6th – – – 29 – –	
		2.20 pm	4th – – – 34 – –	
	22/9	11.15 am	B/81 shelled left Lodge Hollebeke Chateau registration (14 HE)	
		11.35 am	– – Hollebeke Chateau – (6 HE)	
		9. pm	3rd Bty fired Test 28 register (1 HE)	
	23/9	1. am	6th – – – 29 – (1 HE)	
		11.29 am	1st – – – 32 – (1 HE)	
		4 pm – 4.45 pm	4th Bty shelled 33 – fire & support trenches, very effective fire observed (40 HE)	
		4 pm – 4.45 pm	3rd – – house at O4 b 0/3 – large portion destroyed (40 HE)	
		4 pm – 4.45 pm	6th – – 30 register fire and support trenches – parapet badly damaged on front of 50 metres (40 HE)	
		4 pm – 4.45 pm	1st – – 31 and 32 register fire and support trenches – very good effect. (40 HE)	
		6.50 pm	6th Bty fired Test 29 register (1 HE)	

1875 Wt. W593/826 1,000,000 4/15 J.B.C. & A. A.D.S.S./Forms/C. 2118.

Instructions regarding War Diaries and Intelligence Summaries are contained in F. S. Regs., Part II. and the Staff Manual respectively. Title Pages will be prepared in manuscript.

WAR DIARY
or
~~INTELLIGENCE~~ SUMMARY
(Erase heading not required.)

Army Form C. 2118

88

Place	Date	Hour	Summary of Events and Information	Remarks and references to Appendices
	22/9	10 pm	3rd Bty fired Test 29 register (1 H.E.)	
		10.40 pm	6th " " " 28 " "	
		11.10 pm	1st " " " 31 " "	
		12.5 pm	6th " shelled 30 register with very good effect (45 H.E)	
		12.5 pm	3rd " " house O4 b 0/3 – good effect but no direct hits obtained (45 H.E)	
		12.6 pm	4th " " 33 register with good effect (45 H.E)	
		12.6 pm	1st " " 31 + 32 registers " " (45 H.E)	
		1.45 pm	3rd " " 28 " as reprisal (10 H.E)	
		2.47 pm	3rd " fired Test 28 " (1 H.E)	
	24/9	1.35 am	1st " " " 31 " "	
		4.20 am	1st " shelled support trenches 31 and 32 register (45 H.E)	
		4.20 am	3rd " " house and O.P.s at O 4 d 0/3 (45 H.E)	
		4.20 am	4th " " 33 register – fire & support (45 H.E)	
		11.30 am	6th " " 30 " " " (45 H.E)	
		10.50 am	6th " fired Test 30 " (1 H.E)	
		1.3 pm	1st " shelled Trench 31 register as reprisal (7 H.E)	
		1.10 pm	1st " " " " " " (3 H.E)	
		1.16 pm	6th " " " 30 " " " (18 H.E)	
		2.43 pm	3rd " fired Test 28 " (1 H.E)	
		1.15 pm	B/81 shelled Hill 60 for registration (14 H.E)	
		2.15 pm	B/81 " House O4 b 0/3 " (14 H.E)	
		7.31 pm	3rd " fired Test 1.8 register (1 H.E)	
		7.49 pm	3rd " " " 29 " (1 H.E)	
		10.55 pm	3rd " " " 29 " (1 H.E)	
	25/9	2.55 am	3rd " " " 28 " (1 H.E)	
		3.50 am – 5.40 am	3rd Bty shelled O.Ps at O4 b 0/3 (133 H.E)	
		3.50 am – 4.30 am	1st " " C.T.s from I 34 d 4/4 to I 34 d 7/9 (60 H.E) (60 Sh)	
		3.50 am – 4.30 am	6th " " I 35 b 8/7 to I 35 c 10/5	
		3.55 am – 4.30 am	5th " " enemy's Bkes in O4 a 4/4, O4 c 8/0, O5 b 2/6 (96 H.E) (60 Sh)	
		4.58 am – 5.3 am	1st " " 31 and 32 register as reprisal (12 H.E)	
		5.13 am	1st " " " " " (12 H.E)	
		5.40 am	6th " " 35 register " (6 H.E)	

WAR DIARY
or
INTELLIGENCE SUMMARY

(Erase heading not required.)

Army Form C. 2118

89

Instructions regarding War Diaries and Intelligence Summaries are contained in F. S. Regs., Part II. and the Staff Manual respectively. Title Pages will be prepared in manuscript.

Place	Date	Hour	Summary of Events and Information	Remarks and references to Appendices
	25/9	6.7am	6th Bty shelled Trench Mortar in 2nd line trench opposite 30 (16 HE)	
		6.15am	4th " " 34 registn as reprisal (6 HE)	
		6.13am	1st " " 32 " " " (30 HE, 20 Sh)	
		6.20am	4th " " 33+34 " " (40 HE)	
		6.35am	6th " " Wall hiding M.G. 30 registn (11 HE)	
		6.55am	1st " " 32 registn as reprisal (10 HE)	
		9.7am	3rd " " O.Ps at O4 b 0/3 (28 HE)	
		9.29am	2nd " " Bty at O4 c 5/0 as reprisal (40 HE 20 Sh)	
		9.33am	3rd " " " " O4 d 4/4 " " (40 HE 20 Sh)	
		9.53am	5th " " " " O4 d 4/4 " " (10 HE)	
		9.?am	3rd " " " " O4 c 7/5 " (50 HE 10 Sh)	
		10.5am	6th " " Trench mortar 2nd line trench opposite 30 (20 HE)	
		10.5am	5th " " Bty at O4 c 5/0 as reprisal (10 HE)	
		10.10am	4th " " " at I 35 d 7/9 " " (40 HE 20 Sh)	
		10.11am	5th " " " " O5 b 2/6 " " (10 HE)	
		10.17am	3rd " " " " O4 b 9/9 " " (40 HE 20 Sh)	
		10.20am	6th " " " " O5 b 2/6 " " (40 HE 20 Sh)	
		10.32am	3rd " " O Ps at O4 b 0/3 (52 HE)	
		11.11am	2nd " " O Ps at O4 b 0/3 (66 HE)	
		3.35pm	3rd " " O Ps at O4 b 0/3 (31 HE)	
		3.40pm	5th " " Bty O5 b 2/6 as reprisal (30 HE)	
		4.35pm	5th " " " O10 b 5/6 " (40 HE 10 Sh)	
		7.11pm	6th " " " O5 b 2/6 " (20 HE 10 Sh)	
		7.44pm	4th " " " I 35 d 7/9 " (20 HE 10 Sh)	
		7.48pm	3rd " " fired Test 28 registn (1 HE)	
	26/9	3.50pm	2nd " " " 28 " (1 HE)	
		11.8pm	6th " " " 30 " (1 HE)	
		4.27pm	1st " " " 32 " (1 HE)	
		4.40pm	6th " " " 29 " (1 HE)	
		8.47pm	1st " shelled 32 " as reprisal (2 HE)	
		11.46pm	5th " fired Test 27 " (1 HE)	
	27/9	2.30pm	3rd " " " 29 " (1 HE)	
		3.27pm	1st " " " 32 " (1 HE)	
		2.41pm	5th " " " 27 " (1 HE)	
		3.44pm	6th " " " 30 " (1 HE)	

1875 Wt. W593/826 1,000,000 4/15 J.B.C. & A. A.D.S.S./Forms/C. 2118.

Instructions regarding War Diaries and Intelligence Summaries are contained in F. S. Regs., Part II. and the Staff Manual respectively. Title Pages will be prepared in manuscript.

WAR DIARY
or
~~INTELLIGENCE SUMMARY~~
(Erase heading not required.)

Army Form C. 2118

90

Place	Date	Hour	Summary of Events and Information	Remarks and references to Appendices
	27/9	4.8 pm	6" Bty fired Test 29 registers battery buffer (1 HE)	
		4.30 pm	5" - - 27 - (1 HE)	
		9.15 pm	1st - - - 30 - (1 HE)	
		9.45 pm	1st - - - 28 - (1 HE)	
	28/9	4.5 am	5" - - - 27 - (1 HE)	
		11.26 am	6" - - - 29 - (1 HE)	
		12.45 pm	5" - - - 27 - (1 HE)	
		12.48 pm	5" - Shelled - - as reprisal (1 HE)	
		2.8 pm	5" - - - - (3 HE)	
		2.10 pm	4" - - 35 - - left of 2nd line as reprisal (10 HE) (3 HE)	
		3.2 pm	1st - fired Test 32 - (1 HE)	
		5.18 pm	5" - Shelled enemy Transport at O4 d 4/4 (8 HE)	
		6.20 pm	1st - - Trench Mortar 31 register as reprisal (8 HE)	
		11. midnight	1st - fired Test 31 registers (1 HE)	
	29/9	12.10 am	5" - - - 27 - (1 HE)	
		3.55 am	6" - - 29 - (1 HE)	
		3.48 am	5" - on Trench 27 - as reprisal (1 HE)	
		8.30 am	5" - - - 27 - - - - (9 HE)	
		11.15 am	6" - - Test 29 - (1 HE)	
		12.15 pm	4" - at Trench 35 - - (20 HE)	
		5 pm	4" - - shelled ammunition Train (4 HE)	
		5.36 pm	5" - - Test 27 registers (1 HE)	
		5.42 pm	1st - - - 32 - (1 HE)	
		6.14 pm	3rd - - - 28 - (1 HE)	
	30/9	3.4 am	3rd - Shelled 28 - as reprisal (6 HE)	
		8.30 am	4" - - 35 registers (2nd line) as reprisal (8 HE)	
		1.20 pm	5" - - Bty at O5 b 2/7 - CRA's order (24 HE)	
		2.40 pm	3rd - - Trench 38 register as reprisal (6 HE)	
		3 pm	5" - - Bty at O5 b 2/7 CRA's orders (40 HE)	
		3.40 pm	5" - - 27 register as reprisal (9 HE)	
		4.50 pm	5" - - 27 - - - (4 HE)	

1875 Wt. W593/826 1,000,000 4/15 J.B.C. & A. A.D.S.S./Forms/C. 2118.

Instructions regarding War Diaries and Intelligence Summaries are contained in F. S. Regs., Part II. and the Staff Manual respectively. Title Pages will be prepared in manuscript.

WAR DIARY
or
INTELLIGENCE SUMMARY
(Erase heading not required.)

Army Form C. 2118

91

Place	Date	Hour	Summary of Events and Information	Remarks and references to Appendices
	30/9	6.14 pm	5th Bty shelled 27 reports as reprisal (16 HE)	
		6.23 pm	4 " " 33.34.35 " " " (112 HE 102 Sh)	
		6.30 pm	1 " " 30.31.32 " " " (180 HE)	
		6.30 pm	3 " " 28.29. " " " (74 HE)	
		6.35 pm	6 " " 29 " " " (51 HE)	
		6.42 pm	5 " " 27 " " " (16 HE)	
		7.20 pm	3 " " 28 " " " (13 HE)	
		8.55 pm	1 " " Trench Mortar " " (5 HE)	
		7.0 pm	B/81 " 28.29 " " (23 HE) at request from 139th Bde. (Inf.)	
			Losses during month.	
			Killed.	
	25/9		3rd Bty - 1 Gr	
	30/9		6th " - 1 Trumpeter	
	30/9		6th " - 1 Gr	
			Wounded	
	15/9		1st " - 1 Gr	
	6/9		2nd " - 1 Gr	
	25/9		3rd " - 1 Gr	
	30/9		6th " - 1 Bombardier	
	30/9		6th " - 1 Gr (died of wounds on same day in Infirmary Poperinghe)	

O i/c
DAG 3rd Ech
Base

46th Division

October

M03

N

121
7493

War Diary.
of
7th Belgian Regiment Field Artillery,
attached 24th Division

Vol VIII

12

Instructions regarding War Diaries and Intelligence Summaries are contained in F. S. Regs., Part II. and the Staff Manual respectively. Title Pages will be prepared in manuscript.

WAR DIARY
or
~~INTELLIGENCE~~ SUMMARY
(Erase heading not required.)

Army Form C. 2118

92

Place	Date	Hour	Summary of Events and Information	Remarks and references to Appendices
	Oct. 1	6.25 pm	5th Btty fired Test 27 register 1 H.E.	
		6.25 pm	3rd " 28 " 1 H.E.	
	2	8.15 am	1st " shelled working party at O4a 9/8 - 30 H.E. 20 Sh.	
		5 pm	3rd " " point O4a 9/8 as reprisal 41 H.E. 10 Sh	
		8.10 pm	3rd " " 29 register as reprisal 30 H.E. 10 Sh	
		8.45 pm	1st " " 31 " (Trench Mortar) 3 H.E.	
	3	4.45 am	3rd " " 29.32.33 as reprisal 24 H.E.	
		9.27 am	3rd " fired Test 28 register 1 H.E.	
		10.26 pm	5th " shelled 27 " —"— 18 H.E.	
	4	12.54 pm	4th " " 34 " (working party) 4 H.E.	
		1. pm	4th " " 34 " —"— 4 H.E.	
		1.17 pm	4th " " 33.34 " (2nd line) as reprisal 40 H.E.	
		5.48 pm	5th " " 27 " —"— 12 H.E.	
	5	4 pm	1st " " 32 " (Trench Mortar) 59 H.E. 10 Sh	
		4.15 pm	3rd " " 28 " —"— 10 H.E.	
	6	5.55 pm	1st " " 32 " (Trench Mortar) 59 H.E. 10 Sh.	
	7	9.50 am	1st " fired Test 32 " 1 H.E.	
	8	3.33 pm	4th " Shelled 33 " (working party) 13 H.E.	
		4.20 pm	4th " " 34 " as reprisal 22 H.E.	
		4.36 pm	4th " " 34 " —"— 10 H.E.	
	9	10 am	4th " " 34 " —"— 6 H.E.	
	10	8.10 pm	3rd " " 29 " (Trench Mortar) 10 H.E.	
	11	8.30 am	4th " " 34 " as reprisal 12 H.E.	
		8.50 am	1st " " 32 " " 10 H.E.	
		9. am	1st " " 32 " " 5 H.E.	
		2.25 pm	4th " " 34 " " 40 H.E.	
	12	10.30 am	4th " " I 34 b 8/3 (Machine Gun) 12 H.E.	
	13	1.30 pm	3rd " " 28 register " 12 H.E.	
		4 pm	4th " " 34 " " 20 H.E.	

1875 Wt. W593/826 1,000,000 4/15 J.B.C. & A. A.D.S.S./Forms/C. 2118.

Army Form C. 2118

93.

WAR DIARY
or
INTELLIGENCE SUMMARY
(Erase heading not required.)

Instructions regarding War Diaries and Intelligence Summaries are contained in F. S. Regs., Part II. and the Staff Manual respectively. Title Pages will be prepared in manuscript.

Place	Date	Hour	Summary of Events and Information	Remarks and references to Appendices
	Oct 13	5pm	4th Bty shelled enemy Bty at I 35 c 3.5 20 H.E.	
	14	12.47 pm	4th " " " 34 register as reprisal 15 H.E.	
		4 pm	1st " " " 31.32 " " 10 H.E.	
		4.12 pm	4th " " " 34 " " 20 H.E.	
		6.50 pm	1st " " " 32 " " 10 H.E.	
		7.5 pm	4th " " " 34 " " 35 H.E.	
	15	1.30 am	4th " " " 33.34.35 " " 8 H.E.	
		2 am	1st " " " 30 " (Trench mortar) 5 H.E.	
		3 am	4th " " " 33.34.35 " as reprisal 20 H.E.	
		3.10 am	1st " " " 30 " " 5 H.E.	
		3.20 am	1st " " " 30 " " 5 H.E.	
		3.50 am	1st " " " 30 " " 7 H.E.	
		4 am	1st " " " 32 " " 24 H.E.	
		4.12 am	3rd " " " 29 " " 12 H.E.	
		4.20 am	3rd " " " 29 " " 9 H.E.	
		4.30 am	4th " " " 33.34.35 " " 6 H.E.	
		8.50 am	3rd " " " 29 " " 6 H.E.	
		9.5 am	3rd " " " 29 " " 6 H.E.	
		9.29 am	3rd " " " 29 " " 12 H.E.	
		9.55 am	3rd " " " 29 " " 40 H.E. 20 Sh.	
		9.58 am	4th " " " 33 " " 12 H.E.	
		10.5 am	4th " " " 34 " " 10 H.E.	
		12.55 pm	5th " " " 27 " " 8 H.E.	
		1.35 pm	3rd " " " 29 " " 18 H.E.	
		2.35 pm	5th " " " 27 " " 8 H.E.	
	16	5.5 am	4th " " " 33 " " 10 H.E.	
		5.30 am	4th " " " 33.34 " " 20 H.E.	
		5.40 am	4th " " " 34 " " 10 H.E.	
		5.20 am	5th " " " 27 " " 26 H.E.	
		3.16 pm	3rd " " " 29 " " 3 H.E.	
		8. pm	5th " " cross-road at O 11 b 10.7 30 H.E. 42nd Inf. Bde having reported that German	
		8.45 pm	5th " " road from O 10 b 6.5 relief was taking place.	
		9.30 pm	1st " " Support & Comm^n Trenches in front of 30.31 & 32 including road from I 34 d 6/1 to I 34 d 10/6 40 H.E.	
		9.45 pm	3rd " " Trenches from O 4 b 5/8 to O 4 b 9/7 - 30 H.E.	
		10.15 pm	5th " " O 4 c 6/0 to O 4 c 4.4 20 H.E.	

Army Form C. 2118

94

Instructions regarding War Diaries and Intelligence Summaries are contained in F. S. Regs., Part II. and the Staff Manual respectively. Title Pages will be prepared in manuscript.

WAR DIARY
or
INTELLIGENCE SUMMARY
(Erase heading not required.)

Place	Date Oct	Hour	Summary of Events and Information	Remarks and references to Appendices
	17	9.20 am	3rd Bty shelled 29 Register as reprisal 3 H.E.	
		1.40 pm	4th " " 32 " 2nd line " 16 H.E.	
		2.44 pm	5th " " Bty at O 11 b 2.1 " 47 H.E. 10 cm	
		2.55 pm	4th " " 32 register " 12 H.E.	
		8.5 pm	3rd " " 29 " 2 H.E.	
		8.10 pm	3rd " " 29 " " 41 H.E.	
	18	8.30 am	4th " " 32 " for registration 16 H.E.	
		6.12 pm	5th " " Bty in O5 b 5/5 30 H.E.	
	19	4.45 pm	4th " " 32 register as reprisal 6 H.E.	
		5.38 pm	4th " " 32 " 10 H.E.	
		6.15 pm	3rd " " Bty in O4 d 9.9 " 20 H.E.	
		6.10 pm	C/53 " " " " O9 b 5/5 " 20 H.E. on order of Belgian Group (at request of III Div.)	
			one section of C.53 withdrew from position & one section of A109 replaced it.	
	20	2.5 pm	4th Bty shelled 32 register as reprisal 6 H.E.	
		2.15 pm	4th " " 31 " " 8 H.E.	
		2.30 pm	1st " " 30 " " 8 H.E.	
			A109 registered all guns on zero line at O4 b 0.1½ and one gun on enemy trenches in O4 a, the latter caused considerable bombardment of BLOEF and therefore further registration was stopped.	
	21	9 pm	1st Bty shelled 30 register as reprisal 6 H.E.	
		10.30 pm	4th " " 32 " 8 H.E.	
			A109 continued registration of trenches 13 H.E.	
	22	11.30 am	3rd " shelled 28 register as reprisal 12 H.E.	
		2.45 pm	5th " 27 " 8 H.E.	
		8.25 pm	3rd " " working party at Chau MAHIEU. 8 H.E.	
		9.25 pm	3rd " " 28 register as reprisal 10 H.E.	
	23	11.40 am	3rd " fired Test 30 " 1 H.E.	
		11.00 pm	1st " Shelled 30 register 5 H.E.	
		11.35 pm	4th " " 32 10 H.E.	
	24	1.10 pm	4th " " 31 " 10 H.E.	

1875 Wt. W593/826 1,000,000 4/15 J.B.C. & A. A.D.S.S./Forms/C. 2118.

Army Form C. 2118

95

Instructions regarding War Diaries and Intelligence Summaries are contained in F. S. Regs., Part II. and the Staff Manual respectively. Title Pages will be prepared in manuscript.

WAR DIARY
or
~~INTELLIGENCE SUMMARY~~
(Erase heading not required.)

Place	Date Oct	Hour	Summary of Events and Information	Remarks and references to Appendices
	24	6.10 pm	3rd Bty shelled hostile guns at O4 b 8.9 – 30 H.E. 10 Sh.	Result: heavy enemy shelling of our communications (owing probably to their knowledge of relief of III Div by 17th Div) ceased.
		6.10 pm	5th ″ ″ ″ ″ ″ ″ – 30 H.E. 10 Sh	
		6.15 pm	A 109 ″ ″ ″ ″ ″ 15 H.E.	
		6.46 pm	1st ″ ″ 30 register as reprisal 12 H.E.	
	25	3.30 pm	1st ″ ″ 29 ″ ″ 12 H.E.	
		9 pm	4th ″ ″ 31 + 32 ″ ″ 8 H.E.	
	26	11.10 am	1st ″ ″ 29 ″ ″ 5 H.E.	
		11.48 am	1st ″ ″ ″ ″ ″ 4 H.E.	
		3.30 pm	4th ″ ″ Armoured train at I 35 b 6/8 8 H.E.	
			A 109 continued registration of points in enemy lines.	
	27	10.25 am	5th ″ shelled 27 register as reprisal 8 H.E.	
		10.55 am	1st ″ ″ 30 ″ ″ 30 H.E.	
		7.39 pm	4th ″ ″ Armoured train at I 35 b 6/8 50 H.E. 5 sh.	
		8.58 pm	1st ″ ″ 29 register as reprisal 2 H.E.	
		10.58 pm	1st ″ ″ 29 + 30 ″ ″ 12 H.E.	
		11.10 pm	1st ″ ″ 29 + 31 ″ ″ 15 H.E.	
	28	1 am	1st ″ ″ 29 ″ ″ 4 H.E.	
		1.15 am	1st ″ ″ ″ ″ ″ 4 H.E.	
		1.50 am	1st ″ ″ ″ ″ ″ 3 H.E.	
		1.52 am	1st ″ ″ 31 ″ ″ 4 H.E.	
		2.55 am	1st ″ ″ 29 ″ ″ 3 H.E.	
		8.45 am	3rd ″ ″ 28 Test 1 H.E.	
		1.30 pm	1st ″ ″ 31 register ″ 10 H.E.	
		1.35 pm	1st ″ ″ 31 ″ ″ 12 H.E.	
		3.30 pm	4th ″ ″ 32 ″ ″ 5 H.E.	
			A 109 registered points I 34 d 5.5 + 0.3. 25 H.E	
	29	1.35 pm	4th ″ ″ 32 register 8 H.E.	
		3 pm	A 109 registered points I 34 d 0.1 + I 34 d 2½/2	

1875 Wt. W593/826 1,000,000 4/15 J.B.C. & A. A.D.S.S./Forms/C. 2118.

Instructions regarding War Diaries and Intelligence Summaries are contained in F. S. Regs., Part II. and the Staff Manual respectively. Title Pages will be prepared in manuscript.

WAR DIARY
or
~~INTELLIGENCE SUMMARY~~
(Erase heading not required.)

Army Form C. 21[illegible]

96

Place	Date Oct	Hour	Summary of Events and Information	Remarks and references to Appendices
	30	2.30 pm	1st Bty shelled 31 register as reprisal 21 H.E.	
	31	10.4 pm	5th " " Hostile Bty in O11b 9/7. 40 H.E.	
			A109 registered enemy 1st line trench in O4a8.6 10 H.E.	
			Casualties during October.	
	8		Killed (accidently) Dr NEYT - badly hurt when obtaining material in VLAMERTINGE, died in hospital 9.10.15. 1st Battery.	
	6		Wounded - Sgt. DRUEZ 6th Battery.	
	19		" - Sgt. BONDROIT 4th "	

Roilwood
Lt R.A.
for O.C. 7th Belgian Field Arty

Instructions regarding War Diaries and Intelligence Summaries are contained in F. S. Regs., Part II. and the Staff Manual respectively. Title Pages will be prepared in manuscript.

WAR DIARY
or
INTELLIGENCE SUMMARY
(Erase heading not required.)

Army Form C. 2118

92

Place	Date	Hour	Summary of Events and Information	Remarks and references to Appendices
	Oct. 1	6.25p	5th Bty fired Test 27 registn. 1 H.E.	
		[illegible]	1st " " 28 " 1 H.E.	
	2	[illegible] am	1st " shelled working party at O4a 4/8. 30 H.E. 20 Sh.	
		[illegible]	3rd " " [illegible] O4a 6/8 as reprisal 40 H.E. 10 Sh.	
		[illegible]	1st " " 29 registn. as reprisal 30 H.E. 10 Sh.	
		8.4[illegible] p	1st " " 31 " (Trench Mortar) 3 H.E.	
	3	[illegible] am	3rd " " 29 32 33 as reprisal 24 H.E.	
		9.[illegible] am	3rd " fired Test 28 registn. 1 H.E.	
		[illegible] pm	5th " shelled 27 " 18 H.E.	
	4	12.[illegible] pm	4th " " 34 " (working party) 4 H.E.	
		1 pm	4th " " 34 " 4 H.E.	
		[illegible] pm	4th " " 33.34 " (2nd line) as reprisal 40 H.E.	
		[illegible]	5th " " 27 " " 12 H.E.	
	5	4 pm	1st " " 32 " (Trench Mortar) 59 H.E. 10 Sh.	
		[illegible] pm	1st " " 28 " " 10 H.E.	
	6	5.[illegible] pm	1st " " 32 " (Trench Mortar) 57 H.E. 10 Sh.	
	7	9.50 am	1st " fired Test 32 1 H.E.	
	8	3.35 pm	4th " shelled 33 " (working party) 13 H.E.	
		4.20 pm	4th " " 34 " as reprisal 22 H.E.	
		4.35 pm	4th " " 34 " " 10 H.E.	
	9	10 am	4th " " 34 " " 6 H.E.	
	10	8.10 pm	3rd " " 29 " (Trench Mortar) 10 H.E.	
	11	8.20 am	4th " " 34 " as reprisal 12 H.E.	
		8.50 am	1st " " 32 " " 10 H.E.	
		9. am	1st " " 32 " " 5 H.E.	
		2.25 pm	4th " " 34 " " 40 H.E.	
	12	10.20 am	4th " " I 34 b 8/3 (machine gun) " 12 H.E.	
	13	1.30 pm	3rd " " 28 register " 12 H.E.	
		4 pm	4th " " 34 " " 20 H.E.	

Instructions regarding War Diaries and Intelligence Summaries are contained in F. S. Regs., Part II. and the Staff Manual respectively. Title Pages will be prepared in manuscript.

WAR DIARY
or
INTELLIGENCE SUMMARY
(Erase heading not required.)

Army Form C. 2118

93.

Place	Date Oct	Hour	Summary of Events and Information	Remarks and references to Appendices
	13	5 pm	4th Bty shelled enemy Bt at I 35 c 3.5 20 H.E.	
	14	12.41 pm	4th " " 34 reg[?]ts as reprisal 15 H.E.	
		4 pm	1st " " 31.32 " " 10 H.E.	
		4.12 pm	4th " " 34 " " 20 H.E.	
		6.50 pm	1st " " 32 " " 10 H.E.	
		7.5 pm	4th " " 34 " " 35 H.E.	
	15	1.30 am	4th " " 33.34.35 " " 8 H.E.	
		2 am	1st " " 30 " (Trench Mortar) 5 H.E.	
		3 am	4th " " 33.34.35 " as reprisal 20 H.E.	
		3.10 am	1st " " 30 " " 5 H.E.	
		3.20 am	1st " " 30 " " 5 H.E.	
		3.50 am	1st " " 30 " " 7 H.E.	
		4 am	1st " " 32 " " 24 H.E.	
		4.12 am	3rd " " 29 " " 12 H.E.	
		4.20 am	3rd " " 29 " " 9 H.E.	
		4.30 am	4th " " 33.34.35 " " 6 H.E.	
		8.50 am	3rd " " 29 " " 6 H.E.	
		9.5 am	3rd " " 29 " " 6 H.E.	
		9.29 am	3rd " " 29 " " 12 H.E.	
		9.55 am	3rd " " 29 " " 40 H.E. 20 Sh.	
		9.50 am	4th " " 33 " " 12 H.E.	
		10.5 am	4th " " 34 " " 10 H.E.	
		12.35 pm	5th " " 27 " " 8 H.E.	
		1.35 pm	3rd " " 29 " " 18 H.E.	
		2.35 pm	5th " " 27 " " 8 H.E.	
	16	5.5 am	4th " " 33 " " 10 H.E.	
		5.30 am	4th " " 33.34 " " 20 H.E.	
		5.40 am	4th " " 34 " " 10 H.E.	
		5.20 am	5th " " 27 " " 26 H.E.	
		3.16 pm	3rd " " 29 " " 3 H.E.	
		8 pm	5th " " Cross road at O 11 b 10.7 30 H.E. 72nd Inf. Bde having reported that German relief was taking place.	
		8.45 pm	5th " " road from O 10 b 6.5	
		9.30 pm	1st " " Support + Comm.n Trenches in front of 30.31 + 32 including road from I 34 d 0.1 to I 34 d 10/6 40 H.E.	
		9.45 pm	3rd " " Trenches from O 4 b 5/8 to O 4 b 9/7 - 30 H.E.	
		10.15 pm	5th " " O 4 c 6/0 to O 4 c 4.4 20 H.E.	

Instructions regarding War Diaries and Intelligence Summaries are contained in F. S. Regs., Part II. and the Staff Manual respectively. Title Pages will be prepared in manuscript.

WAR DIARY
or
~~INTELLIGENCE SUMMARY~~

(Erase heading not required.)

Army Form C. 2118

94

Place	Date Oct	Hour	Summary of Events and Information	Remarks and references to Appendices
	17	9.20 am	3rd Bty shelled 29 Register as reprisal 3 H.E.	
		1.40 pm	4th " " 32 " 2nd line " 16 H.E.	
		2.44 pm	5th " " Bty at [illegible] 47 H.E. 18 [illegible]	
		2.55 pm	4th " " 32 register " 12 H.E.	
		8.5 pm	3rd " " 29 " " [illegible] H.E.	
		8.10 pm	3rd " " 29 " " 41 H.E.	
	18	8.20 am	4th " " 32 for registration 11 H.E.	
		1.[illegible] pm	5th " " Bty in 05 b 3/5 30 H.E.	
	19	4.45 pm	4th " " 32 register as reprisal 1 H.E.	
		5.[illegible] pm	4th " " 32 " " 10 H.E.	
		6.15 pm	3rd " " Bty in 04 d 4.9 " 30 H.E.	
		[illegible].10 pm	C/53 " " " 09 b 3/5 " 20 H.E. in order of Belgian Group (at request of III Div.)	
			one section of C 53 withdrawn from position & one section of A 109 replaced it.	
	20	2.5 pm	4th Bty shelled 32 register as reprisal 1 H.E.	
		2.15 pm	4th " " 31 " " 8 H.E.	
		[illegible] 30 pm	1st " " 30 " " 8 H.E.	
			A109 registered all guns on zero line at 104 b 0.½ and one gun on enemy trenches in 04 a, the latter caused considerable bombardment of [illegible] and therefore further registration was stopped.	
	21	9 pm	1st Bty shelled 30 register as reprisal 1 H.E.	
		10.30 pm	4th " " 32 " " 8 H.E.	
			A109 continued registration of trenches 13 H.E.	
	22	11.30 am	3rd " shelled 28 register as reprisal 12 H.E.	
		2.45 pm	5th " " 27 " " 8 H.E.	
		[illegible] 25 pm	3rd " " working party at Chau MAHIEU 8 H.E.	
		9.25 pm	3rd " " 28 register as reprisal 12 H.E.	
	23	11.40 am	3rd " fired Test 20 " 1 H.E.	
		4.45 pm	5th " Shelled 20 register 5 H.E.	
		4.55 pm	4th " " 32 " 10 H.E.	
	24	1.10 pm	4th " " 31 " 10 H.E.	

1875 Wt. W593/826 1,000,000 4/15 J.B.C. & A. A.D.S.S./Forms/C. 2118.

Instructions regarding War Diaries and Intelligence Summaries are contained in F. S. Regs., Part II. and the Staff Manual respectively. Title Pages will be prepared in manuscript.

WAR DIARY
or
~~INTELLIGENCE SUMMARY~~
(Erase heading not required.)

Army Form C. 2118

95

Place	Date Oct	Hour	Summary of Events and Information	Remarks and references to Appendices
	24	6.10pm	3rd Bty shelled howitzer guns at O4 b 8 9 – 30 H.E. 10 Sh.	Result: heavy enemy shelling of our communications (owing probably to their knowledge of relief of III Div by 17th Div) ceased.
		6.10pm	5th – – – – – 30 H.E. 10 Sh.	
		6.15pm	A109 – – – – 15 H.E.	
		6.46pm	1st – – 30 register as reprisal 12 H.E.	
	25	3.30pm	1st – – 29 – – 12 H.E.	
		9 pm	4th – – 31 + 32 – – 8 H.E.	
	26	11.10am	1st – – 29 – – 5 H.E.	
		11.48am	1st – – – – – 4 H.E.	
		3.20pm	4th – – Armoured train at I35 b 6/8 8 H.E.	
			A109 continued registration of points in enemy lines.	
	27	10.25am	5th – Shelled 27 register as reprisal 8 H.E.	
		10.55am	1st – – 30 – – 20 H.E.	
		7.39pm	4th – – Armoured train at I 35 b 6/8 50 H.E. 5 Sh.	
		8.53pm	1st – – 29 register as reprisal 2 H.E.	
		10.58pm	1st – – 29 + 30 – – 12 H.E.	
		11.10pm	1st – – 29 + 31 – – 15 H.E.	
	28	1 am	1st – – 29 – – 4 H.E.	
		1.15am	1st – – – – – 4 H.E.	
		1.50am	1st – – – – – 3 H.E.	
		1.52am	1st – – 31 – – 4 H.E.	
		2.55am	1st – – 29 – – 3 H.E.	
		8.45am	3rd – – 28 Test 1 H.E.	
		1.30pm	1st – – 31 register – 10 H.E.	
		1.35pm	1st – – 31 – – 12 H.E.	
		3.30pm	4th – – 32 – – 5 H.E.	
			A109 registered points I34 d 5.5 + 0.3. 25 H.E.	
	29	1.35pm	4th – – 32 register 8 H.E.	
		3 pm	A109 registered points I34 d 0.1 + I34 d 2½/2	

1875 Wt. W593/826 1,000,000 4/15 J.B.C. & A. A.D.S.S./Forms/C. 2118.

Instructions regarding War Diaries and Intelligence Summaries are contained in F. S. Regs., Part II. and the Staff Manual respectively. Title Pages will be prepared in manuscript.

WAR DIARY
or
~~INTELLIGENCE SUMMARY~~
(Erase heading not required.)

Army Form C. 2118

96

Place	Date Oct	Hour	Summary of Events and Information	Remarks and references to Appendices
	30	2.30pm	1st Bty shelled 31 registr as reprisal 21 H.E.	
	31	10.4pm	5th " Hostile Bty in O11b 9/7 40 H.E.	
			A109 registered enemy 1st line trench in O4a 8.6 10 H.E.	
			Casualties during October	
	8		Killed (accidentally) Dr NEYT - badly hurt when obtaining material in VLAMERTINGE, died in hospital 9.10.15. 1st Battery.	
	6		Wounded - Sgt DRUEZ 6th Battery	
	19		" - Sgt BONDROIT 4th "	

1875 Wt. W593/826 1,000,000 4/15 J.B.C. & A. A.D.S.S./Forms/C. 2118.

Army Form C. 2118

97

Instructions regarding War Diaries and Intelligence Summaries are contained in F. S. Regs., Part II. and the Staff Manual respectively. Title Pages will be prepared in manuscript.

WAR DIARY
or
~~INTELLIGENCE SUMMARY~~
(Erase heading not required.)

Place	Date	Hour	Summary of Events and Information	Remarks and references to Appendices
	Nov 1	9.20 pm	6th Bty shelled 29 register (2nd line) in reprisal 6 H.E.	
			A109 registered O4b5.6 5 H.E.	
	2	9.52 pm	5th - HOLLEBEKE VILLAGE — " — 40 H.E.	
		9.58 pm	1st - shelled Trench Mortar in 31 register 5 H.E.	
		10.35 pm	1st - - — " — 5 H.E.	
		11.10 pm	1st - - 29 register (2nd line) — " — 14 H.E.	
		11.27 pm	6th - - 29 register — " — — " — 156 H.E. (enemy were violently bombarding 29 trench where we were repairing parapet damaged by heavy rains, and we were obliged to fire all night, as each time we stopped retaliation they re-commenced.)	
	3	2.45 am	3rd Bty shelled 29 register as reprisal 12 H.E.	
		9.20 am	1st - - 30 - - 4 H.E.	
		9.35 am	1st - - 30 - - 10 H.E.	
		9.50 am	6th - - 29 - (2nd line) Testing buffer of 2 guns 2 H.E.	
		10.10 am	1st - - 30 - as reprisal 10 H.E.	
		2.31 pm	5th - - 27 - Test 1 H.E.	
		8.30 pm	1st - - 30 - - 4 H.E.	
		8.53 pm	1st - - 30 - - 4 H.E.	
		9.40 pm	1st - - 30 - - 6 H.E.	
		10.25 pm	1st - - 30 - - 6 H.E.	
		10.45 pm	1st - - 30 - - 6 H.E.	
		11.35 pm	1st - - 30 - - 6 H.E.	
			A109 - registered points O3b10.1 & O3b8.1 30 H.E.	
	4	4.30 am	1st - shelled 30 register as reprisal 6 H.E.	
		4.35 am	1st - - 30 - - 6 H.E.	
		11. am	A109 - - HOLLEBEKE village - 12 H.E.	
		11.25 am	4th - - 32 register (2nd line) registration 8 H.E.	
		3.5 pm	1st - - 31 - as reprisal 8 H.E.	
		3.45 pm	3rd - - 27 - - 19 H.E.	
		4.10 pm	1st - - 30 - - 6 H.E.	
		4.25 pm	1st - - 30 - - 8 H.E.	
		4.45 pm	3rd - - 27 - - 18 H.E. 6 H.E.	
			5th Bty was obliged to withdraw from advanced position at B31627 on account of flooding of brook BOLLARDBEECK, and was ordered into reserve in the wagon line	

Army Form C. 2118

WAR DIARY
or
~~INTELLIGENCE SUMMARY~~
(Erase heading not required.)

98

Instructions regarding War Diaries and Intelligence Summaries are contained in F. S. Regs., Part II. and the Staff Manual respectively. Title Pages will be prepared in manuscript.

Place	Date	Hour	Summary of Events and Information	Remarks and references to Appendices
	Nov 5	12.10 pm	1st Btz shelled 30 registn as reprisal 6 H.E.	
		2.50 pm	1st " " 31 " " 10 H.E.	
		3.15 pm	1st " " 31 " " 6 H.E.	
		12.10 pm	A109 " 30 " " 8 H.E.	
	6	7.50 am	4th " " 32 " (2nd line) " 12 H.E.	
		11.20 am	1st " " 31 " 8 H.E.	
		1.5 pm	1st " " 31 " " 8 H.E.	
		1.10 pm	1st " " 31 " " 16 H.E.	
	7	3.50 pm	4th " " 32 " " 20 H.E.	
		4.43 pm	6th " " 29 " " 12 H.E.	
		4.45 pm	1st " " 31 " " 20 H.E.	
		4.50 pm	4th " " 32 " " 20 H.E.	
		5.5 pm	4th " " 31 " " 11 H.E.	
	9	9.5 am	4th " " 32 " " 8 H.E.	
		9.15 am	1st " " 31 " " 10 H.E.	
		9.35 am	1st " " 31 " " 10 H.E.	
		3.30 pm	A109 " " HOLLEBEKE VILLAGE. 6 H.E. } Gen DECHESNE'S orders.	
		5 pm	A109 " " " 6 H.E. }	
	10	7.55 am	4th " " 32 registn " 4 H.E.	
		8 am	4th " " 32 " " 6 H.E.	
		8 am	1st " " 31 " " 16 H.E.	
		1.55 pm	4th " " 34 " (I34 b8.0) 24 H.E.	
		11.20 am	A109 " " an enemy 4.2 How Btz at O4 d 9/9 9 H.E. as this Btz was shelling LANKHOF	
		3.25 pm	4th " " 34 registn (I34 b8.0) " 24 H.E.	
		12.30 pm	D107 " registered on zero line at I34 b6.1, one section having arrived at its position at I26 b1.1 on evening of 8th & other section on evening of 9th - fired 31 rounds.	
	11	10 am	A109 shelled HOLLEBIKE VILLAGE as reprisal 12 H.E.	
		2.30 pm	D107 " point I34 d 5.8 for registration 20 Sh.	
		4 pm	1st Btz " 30 registn as reprisal 6 H.E.	
		11.40 pm	1st " " 31 " " 3 H.E.	
		11.45 pm	4th " " " 6 H.E.	

1875 Wt. W593/826 1,000,000 4/15 J.B.C. & A. A.D.S.S./Forms/C. 2118.

Instructions regarding War Diaries and Intelligence Summaries are contained in F. S. Regs., Part II. and the Staff Manual respectively. Title Pages will be prepared in manuscript.

WAR DIARY
or
~~INTELLIGENCE SUMMARY~~
(Erase heading not required.)

Army Form C. 2118

99

Place	Date	Hour	Summary of Events and Information	Remarks and references to Appendices
	Nov 12	11.35am 1st Bty	shelled trench 30 register as reprisal 24 H.E.	
	13	11.30am A109 "	registered points I34d2.4 - 2.6 and I34b6.1	
		11.55am A109 "	shelled road from O4b3.6 - I34d7.1 - retaliation 10 H.E.	
		12 noon D107 "	" I34d5.8 for registration 7 Sh.	
		12.25pm 6th Bty	" 29 register 2nd line as reprisal 24 H.E.	
	14	9 am D107 "	" I34b6.1 (Trench Mortar) H.E. 8 Sh 18 request of trenches.	
		10.35am 3rd "	" 28 register as reprisal 6 H.E.	
		10.55am 3rd "	" 27 " " 12 H.E.	
	15	11.57am 6th "	" 29 " 2nd line " 24 H.E.	
		3.45pm D107 "	" I34b6.1 (Trench Mortar) 2 H.E. 5 Sh	
		6.15pm " "	" O6a4.6 and O6c7.7 20 Sh. combined retaliation scheme	
		5.25pm 1st "	" 31 register as reprisal 10 H.E.	
		5.50pm 1st "	" Bridge at O5b1.4 10 H.E.	
		6.10pm 1st "	" — " — 10 H.E.	
		6.40pm 1st "	" Communication trenches 20 H.E.	
		4.25pm 6th "	" 29 register as reprisal 6 H.E.	
		4.31pm 6th "	" — " — " 24 H.E.	
		5.30pm 4th "	" 32 " 12 H.E.	
		6.10pm 4th "	" O5b4.2 10 H.E.	
		6.15pm 4th "	" roads (O5b2.2 - O5b3.4 - O5b4.6) 20 H.E. — " —	
		6.17pm 6th "	" O5b8.6 — " —	
		6.25pm 6th "	" — " — 11 H.E. — " —	
	16	9.40am 6th "	" O4a10.8 as reprisal 20 H.E. — " —	
		10.15am 1st "	" trenches 29 - 35 registration of new zone 12 H.E.	
		11.30am 1st "	" 31 register as reprisal 43 H.E.	
		1.40pm 3rd "	" 28 " 13 H.E.	
		6 am D107 "	" Trench Mortar at I34b6.1 15 H.E.	
		2pm 4th "	" 33 34 35 register for registration 12 H.E. 20 Sh.	
		2pm 6th "	" 35 " " 24 H.E.	
		3.30pm 1st "	" 32 " " 9 H.E.	
		6.10pm 4th "	" 34 " reprisal 10 H.E.	
		6.15pm 4th "	" 34 6 H.E.	
			6 H.E.	

Army Form C. 2118

10.0.

WAR DIARY
or
INTELLIGENCE SUMMARY
(Erase heading not required.)

Instructions regarding War Diaries and Intelligence Summaries are contained in F. S. Regs., Part II. and the Staff Manual respectively. Title Pages will be prepared in manuscript.

Place	Date	Hour	Summary of Events and Information	Remarks and references to Appendices
	Nov			
	17	10.30 am	6th Bty shelled point I 35 c 6.6 24 HE. road + C.T.s.	
		11.10 am	4th " " 34 register as reprisal 6 HE.	
		11.26 am	4th " " 34 " " 9 HE.	
		12.20 pm	1st " " C.Ts at I 34 d 5.3 24 HE.	
		12.20 pm	3rd " " O 4 b 4.8 24 HE.	
		6.45 pm	4th " " 34 register " 10 HE.	
	18	8.55 am	3rd " " O 4 b 4.8 4 HE.	Polish deserter reported German reliefs passed by this point between these hours
		9.10 am	" " " " 4 HE.	
		9.25 am	" " " " 4 HE.	
		9.40 am	" " " " 4 HE.	
		9.55 am	" " " " 4 HE.	
		10.10 am	" " " " 4 HE.	
		10.25 am	" " " " 4 HE.	
		10.40 am	" " " " 4 HE.	
		9.30 pm	6th " " 30 register 2nd line " 27 HE.	
		9.45 pm	6th " " " " 4 HE.	
		10.00 pm	4th " " 33 " " 3 HE.	
		[illegible] pm	3rd " " 29 " " 10 HE.	
		8.20 pm	3rd " " 29 " " 24 HE.	
		8.50 pm	1st " " 31 " Trench Mortar	
	19	7.10 am	1st " " I 34 d 9.6 4 HE.	
		7.20 am	" " " " 4 HE.	
		7.40 am	" " " " 4 HE.	
		8.10 am	" " " " 4 HE.	
		8.20 am	" " " " 4 HE.	
		8.30 am	" " " " 4 HE.	
		8.40 am	" " " " 4 HE.	
		8.50 am	" " " " 4 HE.	
		9.00 am	" " " " 4 HE.	
		2.20 pm	" " " redoubt at I 34 d 2.5 50 HE.	Large quantities of timber and other material thrown up.
		3 pm	A109 " " " 8 HE.	
		3.20 pm	6th " " Bridge at O 5 a 4.2 16 HE.	
		3.23 pm	6th " " " O 5 a 7.2 16 HE.	
		3.25 pm	6th " " " O 5 b 1.4 16 HE.	
		10.40 pm	4th " " 33 register reprisal 6 HE.	
		10.55 pm	4th " " 35 " 12 HE.	

1875 Wt. W593/826 1,000,000 4/15 J.B.C. & A. A.D.S.S./Forms/C. 2118.

Instructions regarding War Diaries and Intelligence Summaries are contained in F. S. Regs., Part II. and the Staff Manual respectively. Title Pages will be prepared in manuscript.

WAR DIARY
or
~~INTELLIGENCE~~ SUMMARY
(Erase heading not required.)

Army Form C. 2118

101

Place	Date	Hour	Summary of Events and Information	Remarks and references to Appendices
	Nov			
	20	11.20 am	1st Bty shelled M.G. emplacement at I 34 d 1.5 — 50 H.E. good effect observed – 50 yards of parapet destroyed.	
		3 pm	6th - - 30 + 31 2nd line register 24 H.E.	
		9.55 pm	1st - - 32 register as reprisal 24 H.E.	
	21	7.30 am	1st - - 32 - - - 24 H.E.	
		7.55 am	6th - - 30. 31 2nd line register 23 H.E.	
		8.05 am	4th - - 33. 34. 35 - 24 H.E.	
		10.45 am	4th - - I 34 b 8.1 supposed redoubt 22 H.E.	
		11.30 am	1st - - 30 register as reprisal 24 H.E.	
		12. noon	6th - - 30 2nd line - - 4 H.E.	
		2.25 pm	1st - - 32 (Test) 1 H.E.	
		3.25 pm	1st - - 30 - 1 H.E.	
		9 pm	A109 - I 34 d 7.5 - 12 H.E.	
	22	3.32 pm	4th - - 33 register - 10 H.E.	
		3.45 pm	4th - - 34 - - 10 H.E.	
	23	10.50 am	A109 - - O 4 c 7.8 German working party 12 Sh.	
		10.55 am	3rd - - O 4 c 5.8 - 10 H.E.	
		11.13 am	6th - - 30 register 2nd line 24 H.E.	
		12.45 pm	6th - - - - - 6 H.E.	
		1 pm	6th - - - - - 4 H.E.	
		2.20 pm	1st - - 32 - reprisal 48 H.E.	
		2.50 pm	1st - - 32 - - 24 H.E.	
		3.00 pm	1st - - - - 24 H.E.	
		3 pm	6th - - 31 (Trench mortar) - 52 H.E.	
		11.54 pm	1st - - 32 - - 4 H.E.	
		2.45 pm	A109 - - I 34 d 7.5 - 20 H.E.	
	24	8.15 am	4th - - 35 register - 6 H.E.	
		10.10 am	4th - - - - 6 H.E.	
		9 am	6th - - 31 - - 3 H.E.	
		10.10 am	6th - - 31 - - 9 H.E.	
		10.20 am	4th - - 35 - - 6 H.E.	

1875 Wt. W593/826 1,000,000 4/15 J.B.C. & A. A.D.S.S./Forms/C. 2118.

Army Form C. 2118

102

WAR DIARY
or
~~INTELLIGENCE~~ SUMMARY
(Erase heading not required.)

Instructions regarding War Diaries and Intelligence Summaries are contained in F. S. Regs., Part II. and the Staff Manual respectively. Title Pages will be prepared in manuscript.

Place	Date	Hour	Summary of Events and Information	Remarks and references to Appendices
	Nov 24	11 am	4th Bty shelled 35 register as reprisal 32 H.E.	
		11.30 am	4th – – 34 – – 15 H.E.	
		11.55 am	4th – – 34 – (Trench Mortar) 17 H.E.	
		1.10 pm	1st – – 31 – (working party) 10 H.E.	
		1.40 pm	1st – – 31 – – " – 6 H.E.	
		2.20 pm	4th – – 34 – as reprisal 11 H.E.	
		7.5 pm	4th – – 34 – – 6 H.E.	
		9.45 pm	A109 – – a line from O5 d 3.4 – O5 d 10.2. 18 H.E. the flash of a 6" How having been observed by Belgian Officer. Result enemy shelling of H23b ceased.	
	25	1 pm	4th Bty shelled 35 register as reprisal 18 H.E.	
		1.30 pm	1st – – 33 – (registration of new trench) 10 H.E.	
		4.15 pm	4th – – 34 – as reprisal 6 H.E.	
		4.20 pm	1st – – 32 – – 22 H.E.	
		10 am	129th Bty 30th (How) Bde R.F.A. having replaced A109 (24th Div) fired 9 H.E. on its zone as registration	
	26	10.50 am	6th Bty shelled 31 register (working party) 12 H.E.	
		12.50 pm	6th – – 30 – (2nd line) reprisal 12 H.E.	
		1.10 pm	6th – – 30 – – – 12 H.E.	
		1.40 pm	6th – – 30 – – – 12 H.E.	
		2.25 pm	6th – – 31 – (working party) 6 H.E.	
		3.25 pm	to 5 pm 4th Bty – 35 – retaliation 60 H.E.	
		5 pm	6th Bty – 35 – (2nd + 3rd lines) 24 H.E.	
		5 pm	129th How Bty shelled 35 register (3rd line) heavy enemy Trench Mortar having caused several casualties in our trench 35. 10 H.E.	
		8 .. pm	129 Bty searched for 13 c.m. H.V. gun believed to be firing from armoured train at point I36 c 4.7 12 H.E.	
	27	9.40 am	1st Bty shelled 32 register as reprisal 12 H.E.	

1875 Wt. W593/826 1,000,000 4/15 J.B.C. & A. A.D.S.S./Forms/C. 2118.

Instructions regarding War Diaries and Intelligence Summaries are contained in F. S. Regs., Part II. and the Staff Manual respectively. Title Pages will be prepared in manuscript.

WAR DIARY
or
~~INTELLIGENCE SUMMARY~~
(Erase heading not required.)

Army Form C. 2118

103

Place	Date Nov	Hour	Summary of Events and Information	Remarks and references to Appendices
	27	10.20 am	3rd Bty shelled point O4 d 2.7 (26 registr) 12 H.E.	
		1.5 pm	6th " " 20 registr 2nd line as reprisal 10 H.E.	
	28	10.25 am to 11.35 am	11th " " 34 + 35 " as reprisal 72 H.E.	
	29	12.25 pm	3rd " " 28 registr (working party) 12 H.E. 4 rounds reported dropped right into trench.	
		3.15 pm	1st " " 32 " as reprisal 4 H.E.	
	30	1.45 pm	1st " " C.Ts from I34 d 1.9 - I35 c 1.9. 20 H.E. In accordance with CRA III Div scheme of 27.11.15. for destruction of network of trenches opposite our trench 35, in conjunction with 9.2", 8" and 6" howitzers of 2nd H.A.R.	
		1.45 pm	4th Bty shelled C.Ts from I34 d 5.8 - I34 d 6.7 20 H.E.	In conjunction with above scheme.
		2.7 pm	4th " " —— ditto —— 20 H.E.	
		1.45 pm	6th " " C.Ts from I35 c 1.9 - I35 c 5.6. 20 H.E.	
		2.7 pm	6th " " —— ditto —— 20 H.E.	
			Belgian observers reported heavy howitzer shelling accurate + effective, and that it caused an explosion in enemy trenches.	
		2.7 pm	1st Bty shelled C.Ts from I34 a d.7 - I35 c 7.9 30 H.E.	
		2.20 pm	1st " " 32 registr as reprisal 7 H.E.	
		2.40 pm	1st " " 32 " " 6 H.E.	
		3.15 pm	1st " " 32 " " 6 H.E.	
		4.10 pm	4th " " 34 " " 6 H.E.	
		7 pm	129th " " HOLLEBEKE village " 8 H.E.	
		9.20 pm	1st " " C.Ts opposite 33 trench " 8 H.E. 24 H.E.	
		9.25 pm	129th " " I34 a 6.7 " 12 H.E.	

1875 Wt. W593/826 1,000,000 4/15 J.B.C. & A. A.D.S.S./Forms/C. 2118.

Instructions regarding War Diaries and Intelligence Summaries are contained in F. S. Regs., Part II. and the Staff Manual respectively. Title Pages will be prepared in manuscript.

WAR DIARY
or
~~INTELLIGENCE SUMMARY~~
(Erase heading not required.)

Army Form C. 2118

104

Place	Date	Hour	Summary of Events and Information	Remarks and references to Appendices
	Nov. 30	10 pm	4th Bty shelled 35 register as reprisal 6 HE.	
		1050 pm	4th " " from I 34 d 7.9 to I 35 c 1.9 as reprisal 48 HE.	
			Map referred to YPRES. Sheet 28. 1/20,000	
			Hd. 2trs of 7th Regiment Belgian Field Artillery H.23 b 5.5. attached III Division.	
			Division on our left 9th Div. On our right Canadian Div	
			Casualties during November.	
	4		DELMEZ. M. Stretcher Bearer - 6th Bty. Wounded.	
	11		FAYHAY. H. No 1909. Gunner - 3rd " Wounded.	
			LACROIX. A. Gunner - 3rd " Wounded.	
	16		BORREY A. Gunner - 6th " Wounded.	

1875 Wt. W593/826 1,000,000 4/15 J.B.C. & A. A.D.S.S./Forms/C. 2118.

Instructions regarding War Diaries and Intelligence Summaries are contained in F. S. Regs., Part II. and the Staff Manual respectively. Title Pages will be prepared in manuscript.

WAR DIARY
or
INTELLIGENCE SUMMARY
(Erase heading not required.)

Army Form C. 2118

Place	Date	Hour	Summary of Events and Information	Remarks and references to Appendices
			War Diary (Carbon Duplicates) of 7th Belgian Field Artillery for months of September 1915	
			October ✓	
			November ✓	
			December ✓	
			Noël Wood Lieut. R.A. Liaison Officer.	

1875 Wt. W593/826 1,000,000 4/15 J.B.C. & A. A.D.S.S./Forms/C. 2118.

Army Form C. 2118

105

Instructions regarding War Diaries and Intelligence Summaries are contained in F. S. Regs., Part II. and the Staff Manual respectively. Title Pages will be prepared in manuscript.

WAR DIARY
or
~~INTELLIGENCE SUMMARY~~

(Erase heading not required.)

Place	Date Dec	Hour	Summary of Events and Information	Remarks and references to Appendices
	1	10.10 am	4th Bty shelled 35 register as reprisal 4 H.E.	
		10.35 am	4th Bty – 34 – (Trench Mortar) 48 H.E.	
		12.15 pm	6th – – I.34.d.2.6 (suspected emplacement of Cupola) 44 H.E.	
		12.35 pm	3rd – – 29 register as reprisal 6 H.E.	
		1.5 pm	6th – – 30 – (2nd line) – 34 H.E.	
		1.30 pm	1st – – 32 – – 6 H.E.	
	2	8 am	4th – – 35 – – 12 H.E.	
		8 am	1st – – 32 – – 3 H.E.	
		8.35 am	129th How Bty – 34 – – 12 H.E.	
		8.45 am	6th Bty – 34 – –"– – 21 H.E.	
		10 am	1st – – 33 – (Trench mortar) – 24 H.E.	
		10.5 am	4th – – 34 – –"– 24 H.E.	
		10.20 am	1st – – 32 – – 24 H.E.	
		10.30 am	1st – – 32 – – 9 H.E.	
		10.35 am	4th – – 34 – –"– – 24 H.E.	
		11.30 am	1st – – 33 – – 9 H.E.	
		12.20 pm	1st – – 33 – – 5 H.E.	
		1 pm	6th – – I.34.b.7.1 (supposed bomb-store) 24 H.E.	
		1.40 pm	1st – – 33 register as reprisal 9 H.E.	
		2.35 pm	1st – – 33 – – 11 H.E.	
		3.40 pm	4th – – 34 – – 12 H.E.	
		4.35 pm	1st – – 32 – – 12 H.E.	
	3	5.35 pm	6th – – 30 – – 27 H.E.	
		11 pm	129 How Bty – 29 – – 8 H.E.	
		11 pm	3rd Bty – 29 – (2nd line) – 20 H.E.	
		11.15 pm	6th – – O.4.b.3.9 – – 20 H.E.	

Instructions regarding War Diaries and Intelligence Summaries are contained in F. S. Regs., Part II. and the Staff Manual respectively. Title Pages will be prepared in manuscript.

WAR DIARY
or
INTELLIGENCE SUMMARY
(Erase heading not required.)

Army Form C. 2118

106.

Place	Date	Hour	Summary of Events and Information	Remarks and references to Appendices
	Dec 4	9.30 am	6th Bty shelled point 04 a 9.8 — 50 H.E.	Combined shoot in conjunction with Heavy Howitzers by order of C.R.A. III Div on suspected mine-shaft opposite 29 Trench.
		9.30 am	3rd " " — " — 50 H.E.	
		9.30 am	129 How Bty " — " — 30 H.E.	
		11.15 am	4th Bty " 34 register (Trench Mortar) 24 H.E.	
		12.45 pm	6th " " point I34d2.6 (Cupola) 38 H.E.	
		2.30 pm	1st " " 32 register as reprisal 8 H.E.	
		3.27 pm	6th " " M.G. at I34 c 9½.4½ " 23 H.E.	
		3.35 pm	4th " " I34d0.3 registration 5 H.E.	
		3.40 pm	6th " " M.G. at I34 c 9½.4½ " 10 H.E.	
		9.20 pm	4th " " 35 register (Trench Mortar) 24 H.E.	
		9.53 pm	1st " " 33 " as reprisal 4 H.E.	
		10.15 pm	4th " " 34 " (Trench Mortar) 24 H.E.	
		10.25 pm	4th " " 34 " — " — 12 H.E.	
	5	12.15 am	4th " " 35 " — " — 7 H.E.	
		2.10 am	3rd " " 29 " (working party) 24 H.E.	
		2.55 am	4th " " 34 " (Trench Mortar) 5 H.E.	
		3 am	1st " " 33 " as reprisal 9 H.E.	
		10.45 am	1st " " 33 " (Trench Mortar) 24 H.E.	
		6.10 pm	3rd " " 29 " working party 28 H.E.	
		6.45 pm	1st " " 32 " (Trench Mortar) 24 H.E.	
		6.55 pm	4th " " 34 " — 24 H.E.	
	6	1.5 pm	3rd " " 29 " reprisal 23 H.E.	
		3 pm	6th " " I34d2.4 registration 7 H.E.	
		7.00 pm	3rd " " 29 Trench reprisal 6 H.E.	
		7.45 pm	4th " " 34 " " 24 H.E.	
		8.35 pm	4th " " 34 " " 6 H.E.	
		8.45 pm	4th " " 34 " " 15 H.E.	
		8.40 pm	1st " " 33 " " 15 H.E.	

1875 Wt. W593/826 1,000,000 4/15 J.B.C. & A. A.D.S.S./Forms/C. 2118.

Instructions regarding War Diaries and Intelligence Summaries are contained in F. S. Regs., Part II. and the Staff Manual respectively. Title Pages will be prepared in manuscript.

WAR DIARY
or
INTELLIGENCE SUMMARY
(Erase heading not required.)

Army Form C. 2118

107

Place	Date	Hour	Summary of Events and Information	Remarks and references to Appendices
	Dec 7	11.5 pm	129 How Bty shelled trenches from I34d 2.6 – 03 – 8 H.E.	
		2.25 pm	6th Bty shelled M.G. at I34c 9½ – 4½ as reprisal – 17 H.E. (violent enemy retaliation)	
		2.50 pm	129 How Bty shelled hostile Bty at O11 b 1.1 as reprisal – 20 H.E.	
	8	1.5 pm	1st Bty shelled 33 register as reprisal 10 H.E.	
		3 pm	6th " " pumping operations at I34c 9½.4 55 H.E.	
		3. pm	129 " registered cross roads at HOLLEBEKE 8 H.E. result unsatisfactory, aeroplane messages being confused, as observer tried to register 2 batteries at once.	
		9.45 pm	3rd Bty shelled 29 Support register as reprisal 11 H.E.	
		9.50 pm	3rd " " Bridge at O5a 4.2 49 H.E. } Combined retaliation for hostile shelling of roads in Square H23.	
		9.55 pm	4th " " I35a 4.2 (C.T.s) 48 H.E. }	
		10 pm	129 " " HOLLEBEKE village 20 H.E. }	
	9	10.55 am	4th " " Trench Mortar at trench 35 register 24 H.E.	
		11.25 am	3rd " " Dug-out at O4a 10.9. Initiative 24 H.E.	
		2.45 pm	1st " " first line hostile trench from I34c 10.6 – I34d 2.7. 60 H.E. and then fired 6 salvoes rapid fire at C.T.s & 2nd line from I34d 1.3 – 36 24 H.E.	
		2.45 pm	6th Bty shelled enemy first line from I34c 9.4 – I34c 10.6. 60 H.E. and then fired 6 salvoes on 2nd line trench from I34d 1.3 – 36 23 H.E.	
			76th Infantry Bde report that enemy are living in their front line, the 2nd line having become untenable by reprisals of Belgian batteries. Arrangements have therefore been made with B.M. of Infantry Bde to have our trenches vacated at various times & to retaliate on enemy first line.	
		3.15 pm	4th Bty shelled [illegible] at I34b 6.2 as reprisal 24 H.E.	
		3.40 pm	3rd " " Trench 29 register as reprisal 12 H.E.	
	10	2.15 pm	6th " " " 30 " 4 H.E.	
	11	4.55 am	1st " retaliated H 30 H.E. } H representing areas to be shelled, as retaliation for hostile shelling of a zone within our lines.	See 3rd Div Retaliation Scheme of 2/12/15.
		4.55 am	3rd " " H 30 H.E. }	
		5.10 am	1st " " H 30 H.E. }	
		5. am	129 How Bty " H 16 H.E. }	

1875 Wt. W593/826 1,000,000 4/15 I.B.C. & A. A.D.S.S./Forms/C. 2118.

Instructions regarding War Diaries and Intelligence Summaries are contained in F. S. Regs., Part II. and the Staff Manual respectively. Title Pages will be prepared in manuscript.

WAR DIARY
or
INTELLIGENCE SUMMARY
(Erase heading not required.)

Army Form C. 2118

108

Place	Date	Hour	Summary of Events and Information	Remarks and references to Appendices
	Dec 11	2.15 pm	4th Bty shelled point I35 c 1.9 as reprisal 48 H.E.	
		4 pm	129 How Bty shelled HOLLEBEKE VILLAGE – 12 H.E.	
	12	10.10 am	4th Bty – 35 register, Trench mortar, 24 H.E.	
		10.2 pm	4th – " – – " – 24 H.E.	
		11.40 am	129 How Bty endeavoured to register on HOLLEBEKE cross-roads with aeroplane, but clouds prevented observation. 2 H.E.	
		1.15 pm	4th Bty shelled Trench mortar in 34 register, as reprisal, 24 H.E.	
		1.15 pm	1st 32 register 20 H.E.	
		8 pm	129 How Bty – point O 11 a 6 8½ as reprisal for hostile shelling of square H23. 16 H.E.	
	13	9.20 am	4th Bty shelled from I34 b 6.1 – I34 d 7.9 20 H.E.	
		9.20 am	1st – – C.T.s from I34 d 4.9 – 6.7 30 H.E.	
		9.30 am	1st – – – " – 30 H.E.	
		9.30 am	4th – – I34 b 6.1 – I34 d 7.9 20 H.E.	
		9.45 am	3rd – – Dug-out at O 4 a 2.3 30 H.E. direct hit obtained.	
		10.30 am	4th – – I34 b 6.1 – I34 d 7.9	
		10.30 am	1st – – C.T.s from I34 b 6.1 – I34 d 7.9 25 H.E.	
		10.30 am	129 How Bty – points I34 d 6.7 – 7.9 25 H.E. 20 H.E.	
			The above shoots were part of a combined bombardment ordered by C.R.A. III Div in conjunction with 9.2, 8" and 6" Hows on enemy trenches opposite 33 & 34. Observers reported great damage inflicted – large quantities of sand-bags & planks were blown into the air and a gap 5 yards wide made in 1st line parapet at I34 d 4.9.	
		10.36 am	6th Bty shelled point I34 d 7.5 as reprisal 31 H.E.	
		1.20 pm	6th – – trench 32	
		4.40 pm	1st – – – – 7 H.E.	
		4.55 pm	1st – – – 33 – 13 H.E.	
		8.5 pm	4th – – Point I35 c 1.9 Trench mortar 10 H.E.	
	14	7.45 am	6th – – working party at I30 d 4.4 24 H.E.	
		10.10 am	6th – – – " – 5 H.E.	
		4.30 pm	6th – – – " – trench 30 registr. 12 H.E.	
		5.45 pm	1st – – Chateau O 4 9 [illegible] 9 H.E. 40 H.E.	

Instructions regarding War Diaries and Intelligence Summaries are contained in F. S. Regs., Part II. and the Staff Manual respectively. Title Pages will be prepared in manuscript.

WAR DIARY
or
~~INTELLIGENCE SUMMARY~~
(Erase heading not required.)

Army Form C. 2118

109.

Place	Date	Hour	Summary of Events and Information	Remarks and references to Appendices
	Dec 14th	6 pm	3rd Bty shelled Chateau O4d retaliation 40 H.E.	
		6 pm	129 How Bty " O11a 6.8½ Hostile Bty 20 H.E.	
		6.5 pm	6th Bty " Chateau O4d retaliation 40 H.E.	
		12 midt	3rd " " Bridge O4a 7.7 12 H.E. request of Infy Bn.	
	15	6.45 am	1st " " 32 register reprisals 5 H.E.	
		7 am	3rd " " Bridge O4a 7.7 12 H.E. —"—	
		7.15 am	1st " " 32 register —"— 15 H.E.	
	15	9.5 am	6th " " I34d 1.5 New enemy work 6 H.E.	
		5 pm	3rd " " O4b 2.6 reprisals 50 H.E.	
		5 pm	3rd " " I34a 7.2 —"— 48 H.E.	
		5 pm	129 How Bty " HOLLEBEKE village " 20 H.E.	
		5.5 pm	1st Bty " I34 a 10.6 " 48 H.E.	
	16	1 am	3rd " " 29 register " 24 H.E.	
		12.15 pm	129 How Bty " O5b 6.7 - 6.8 & O6a 0.1 retaliation H 16 H.E.	
		12.15 pm	1st Bty " I35c 2.1 - O5a 4.9 —"— 30 H.E.	
		12.35 pm	3rd " " O5a 2.3 - 6.3 —"— 30 H.E.	
		12.45 pm	4th " " I35c 5.6 - 8.4 —"— 30 H.E.	
		12.35 pm	6th " " O5b 0.5 - 6.7 —"— 30 H.E.	
		12.55 pm	4th " " I35b 6.4 (armoured train) 30 H.E.	
			above retaliation was carried out at the request of the 76th Infy Bde, as enemy were heavily shelling behind our Trenches. The 6th Bty had an officer severely wounded, & 2nd Bty a gun buried, but undamaged, and an amm. wagon destroyed. Otherwise very little damage done.	
		1 pm	129 How Bty registered point I34d 0.3 9 H.E.	
		3 pm	3rd Bty shelled O4a 6.6 reprisal 6 H.E.	
		9.5 pm	4th " " 34 register (Trench Mortar) 24 H.E.	
		9.15 pm	1st " " 33 " reprisal 10 H.E.	
		9.40 pm	4th " " 34 " " 10 H.E.	
		9.45 pm	1st " " 32 " " 10 H.E.	
		9.50 pm	4th " " 34-35 " " 10 H.E.	

Instructions regarding War Diaries and Intelligence Summaries are contained in F. S. Regs., Part II. and the Staff Manual respectively. Title Pages will be prepared in manuscript.

WAR DIARY
or
~~INTELLIGENCE SUMMARY~~
(Erase heading not required.)

Army Form C. 2118

110

Place	Date	Hour	Summary of Events and Information	Remarks and references to Appendices
	Dec 17	10 a.m.	6th Bty shelled front line enemy trench from I 34 d 1.3 – 0.2 . 60 H.E.	
		10 a.m.	8th " " " " " I 34 c 9.1 – d 0.2 61 H.E.	
		10.45 am	11th " " 34 register (Trench Mortar) 24 H.E.	
		11 am	129 " " front line enemy trench from I 34 d 1.3 – c 9.1 30 H.E.	
			The above was a combined shoot in which 1 gun of the 3rd Siege Bty cooperated, with object of destroying any gas reservoirs in enemy front line. In compliance with X Corps Order C.R. 4002.	15/12/15.
		3.20 pm	4th Bty shelled 35 register (Trench Mortar) 24 H.E.	
		4.15 pm	4th " " enemy transport behind 34 register 12 H.E.	
		7.50 pm	1st " " 32 register reprisal 24 H.E.	
		8.30 pm	1st " " —"— (Trench Mortar) 24 H.E.	
		9.7 pm	1st " " —"— —"— 24 H.E.	
		9.40 pm	4th " " 34 register —"— 10 H.E.	
	18	11.30 am	6th " " trenches at I 34 d 1.5 27 H.E.	
		1.5 pm – 2.35 pm	4th Bty " 34 & 35 register reprisal 96 H.E.	
		5.5 pm	6th " " 30 register (2nd line) " 25 H.E.	
		5.30 pm	6th " " —"— " 24 H.E.	
		5.55 pm	1st " " 32 —"— " 13 H.E.	
		7.20 pm	1st " " —"— " 18 H.E.	
		8 pm	1st " " 32 (Trench Mortar) 24 H.E.	
		8.25 pm	1st " " 32 & 33 11 H.E.	
		9.2 pm	129 How " " O 11 b 4½.5 (Howitzer Bty) 15 H.E.	
		9.5 pm	2nd " " O 4 b central —"— 20 H.E.	
	19	4 am – 6 am	1st " " 32 & 33 register reprisal 192 H.E.	
		4.15 am – 6.30 am	3rd " " 29/30 & 31 " 100 H.E.	
		5 am	6th " " 34 & 37 " 44 H.E.	
		5.?am – 6 am	4th " " I 34 d 2.4 " 129 H.E.	
		6 am	129 How " " 19 H.E.	

Instructions regarding War Diaries and Intelligence Summaries are contained in F. S. Regs., Part II. and the Staff Manual respectively. Title Pages will be prepared in manuscript.

WAR DIARY
or
~~INTELLIGENCE SUMMARY~~
(Erase heading not required.)

Army Form C. 2118

111.

Place	Date Dec	Hour	Summary of Events and Information	Remarks and references to Appendices
	19		above shoots were occasioned by the fact that enemy began heavily bombarding our Trenches & batteries at 6 am - the latter with a large number of gas shells. At the same time opening heavy rifle fire. No Infantry attack took place on our trenches, nor on our flanks. Gas did no damage.	
		11.15 am	129 How Bty shelled from O4 a 9.9 - I34 c 9½-1½ 50 H.E.	
		11.30 am	6th Bty " " I34 d ½.3 - I34 c 9.1 100 H.E.	
		11.30 am	3rd " " " I34 c 9.1 - E N. edge of Canal 99 H.E.	
		11.40 am	2nd " " " O4 b 3.6 - O4 a 8.8 40 H.E.	
			above shoot was on front line parapet in conjunction with 8" & 6" hows, organised by 2nd D.A. Result was good. I Corps Order G.X. 4002 of 15.12.15.	
		11.50 am	4th Bty shelled 34 registn reprisal 24 H.E.	
		11.55 am	1st " " 33 " 12 H.E.	
		3.15 pm	4.30 pm 129 Bty " line I34 d 7.9 - 44 including retaliation F. & G. 61 H.E.	
		3.45 pm	4.45 pm 1st " " 32 + 33 registn as reprisal 339 H.E.	
		3.50 pm	4.40 pm 4th " " 34 + 35 + 30 rds on 37 (supporting 51st Bde R.F.A. reprisals 253 H.E.	
		4 pm	4.45 pm 6th " " 30 + 31 registn reprisal 99 H.E.	
		10.35 pm	4th Bty " 34 " 10 H.E.	
	20	12.5 am	4th " " I34 b 7.2 (Trench mortar) 12 H.E.	
	19	4.15 pm	1st " " 32, 33 registn 60 H.E.	
		4.15 pm	3rd " " 29 " 20 H.E.	
		4.15 pm	2nd " " 34 " 86 H.E.	
	20	1.15 pm	4th " " 34 + 35 " 48 H.E.	
		3.20 pm	4th " " 34 " 20 H.E.	
		6 pm	4th " " 34 " 12 H.E.	
	21	2 pm	2nd " fired 31 rounds adapted ammunition (H.E.) on O4 d 1.8, as a trial, result was normal & good.	
	22	6 am - 7 am	2nd Bty shelled O4 b 3-6 - I34 d 7.1 20 H.E. 30 Sh	Combined shoot ordered by CRA 2nd Div on enemy Communications & roads.
		6 am - 7 am	1st " " I34 d 7.1 - I35 c 2.8 20 H.E. 30 Sh	
		6 am - 7 am	4th " " I35 c 2.8 - I35 a 4.2 - I35 c 4.8 20 H.E. 30 Sh	
		6 am - 7 am	6th " " I35 c 4.8 - I35 d 9½.0 20 H.E. 30 Sh	
		6 am - 7 am	129 How Bty " O5 a 8.5 15 H.E. 10 Sh	

Instructions regarding War Diaries and Intelligence Summaries are contained in F. S. Regs., Part II. and the Staff Manual respectively. Title Pages will be prepared in manuscript.

WAR DIARY
or
~~INTELLIGENCE SUMMARY~~
(Erase heading not required.)

Army Form C. 2118

112

Place	Date	Hour	Summary of Events and Information	Remarks and references to Appendices
	Dec 22	9.45 am	129 Bty shelled from C4 a 9.9 - I34 c 9.1 50 H.E.	
		9.45 am	3rd " " " 29 front line enemy trench 99 H.E.	
		9.45 am	6th " " " I34 d 1.3 - I34 c 9.1 100 H.E.	
		10.? am	1st " " " I34 d 0.1 - O4 b 4.8 (C.Ts) 30 H.E.	
		10.30 am	9th " " C.Ts behind 29 register 30 H.E.	
			above was a combined shoot with 8" + 6" Hows on enemy front line, which had been repaired since bombardment of 19/12/15. Result was v.g. Seven breaches were seen in parapet + wire badly blown about.	
	23	9 am to 10.30 pm	4th Bty shelled 34 + 35 register (Trench Mortar) 84 H.E.	
		2.15 pm	129 How Bty " HOLLEBEKE cross roads 16 H.E.	
		4.5 pm	4th Bty " I35 a 2½ 4½ (enemy O.P.) 40 H.E.	
	24	? 45 am	4th " " 35 register (Trench Mortar) 24 H.E.	
		1.10 pm	1st " " working party opp. 32 10 H.E.	
		5 pm 7 pm	4th " " 34 register as reprisal 16 H.E.	
		? pm	This Bty was bombarded by a section of 6" hows, and a direct hit on a dug-out killed Lieutenant SCHIEVEKAMP, a valued Belgian Officer	
	26	? pm	4th Bty shelled from I34 b 8.2 - I34 d 6.7 40 H.E.	
		? pm	3rd " " 29 register - 2nd line - 40 H.E.	
		?.5 pm	4th " " 34 " as reprisal 24 H.E.	
		? pm	6th " " from I34 c 9½ 5 - I34 d 0.7 and I34 d 1.4 - I34 d ½ 3. 105 H.E. 21 Sh	}
		? pm	1st " " I34 d 2.7 & I34 d 0.7 75 H.E.	}
		?.5 pm	129 How Bty - " I34 d 0.3 - 0.7 20 H.E.	}
		? pm	129 " " " I34 d 0.3 - 2.5 20 H.E.	}
		? pm	1st Bty " " I34 d 2.5 - 1.4 30 H.E. 20 Sh	}
			above was combined shoot with 8" + 6" hows, ordered by C.R.A. 2nd Div on enemy front line. Result was good.	
	27	9.45 am	3rd Bty shelled working party at I34 c 9.1. 5 H.E.	
		? pm	3rd " " " 14 H.E.	
		? pm	3rd " " behind 31 register 28 H.E.	
		3 pm	129 How " " O4 b 5.3 (Hostile Bty) 20 H.E.	

1875 Wt. W593/826 1,000,000 4/15 J.B.C. & A. A.D.S.S./Forms/C. 2118.

Instructions regarding War Diaries and Intelligence Summaries are contained in F. S. Regs., Part II. and the Staff Manual respectively. Title Pages will be prepared in manuscript.

WAR DIARY

or

~~INTELLIGENCE SUMMARY~~

(Erase heading not required.)

Army Form C. 2118

113

Place	Date Dec	Hour	Summary of Events and Information	Remarks and references to Appendices
	28	11.5am	129 How Bty shelled working party at I 34 d 4.5 — 8 H.E.	
		11.30am	1st Bty shelled 32 register as reprisal — 11 H.E.	
		11.45am	129 How Bty – 33 – (Trench Mortars) — 10 H.E.	
		11.50am	1st – – 32 – as reprisal — 12 H.E.	
		2 pm	6th – – house at I 34 d 2.4 – registration — 25 H.E.	
		2 pm	1st – – MG emplacement at I 34 d 7.9 — 40 H.E.	
			13 direct hits obtained – stretcher bearers observed to approach & were shelled.	
		3.5pm	1st Bty shelled working party at I 34 d 7.9 — 6 H.E.	
		4.15pm	4th – – 34 register as reprisal — 12 H.E.	
	29	[illegible]	5th – – working party 31 register — 10 H.E.	
		[illegible]	3rd – – O 4 a 7.2 – O 4 b 7.8 — 100 H.E.	
		[illegible]	129 How Bty – —"— — 30 H.E.	
		[illegible]	6th – – —"— — 101 H.E.	
		[illegible]	3rd – – 29 register as reprisal — 24 H.E.	
		4.15pm	1st – – 32 – (Trench Mortar) — 24 H.E.	
		[illegible]	1st – – 32 – — 7 H.E.	
		5.45pm	1st – – 32 – — 2 H.E.	
		5.55pm	4th – – 35 – —"— — 24 H.E.	
	30	8.10am	6th – – working party 31 register (2nd line) — 22 H.E.	
		9.?am	1st – – enemy transport at I 35 a 4.2 — 6 H.E.	
		1.30pm	129 How – – O 4 b 2.9 Trench Mortar — 36 H.E.	
		1.?pm	3rd – – 29 register as reprisal — 29 H.E.	
			O 11 b 7.8 Hostile Bty — 60 H.E.	
		3.?pm	129 How – – line I 34 d 6½.8 – 7.9 – I 35 c 1.9 & I 35 c 8.8 — 60 H.E. }	
		9.15am	129 – – C.T.s from I 34 b 5.0 to I 34 d 9.7½ — 80 H.E. }	
		9.15am	1st Bty – C.T.s – I 34 d 6.7 – 9.3 — 50 H.E. }	
		10.?am	6th –	
			above was part of combined shoot with 2 H.A.R. on enemy front line & C.Ts. Result: no considerable damage to enemy parapet could be observed.	

Instructions regarding War Diaries and Intelligence Summaries are contained in F. S. Regs., Part II. and the Staff Manual respectively. Title Pages will be prepared in manuscript.

WAR DIARY
or
~~INTELLIGENCE SUMMARY~~
(Erase heading not required.)

Army Form C. 2118

114

Place	Date 1915 Dec	Hour	Summary of Events and Information	Remarks and references to Appendices
	31	10.35	4th Bty shelled 34 [illegible] as reprisal 24 H.E.	
		10.[illegible] am	1st " " 33 " 24 H.E.	
		2 pm	4th " " C.T.s from I 34 b 8 1 - I 35 a 1.1 20 H.E.	
		2 pm	1st " " " I 34 b 8 1 - I 35 a 1.1 20 H.E.	
		3.5 pm	1st " " 3[illegible] [illegible] Trench mortar 24 H.E.	
		11 pm	6th " " I 34 d 4½ - 4½ 40 H.E.	
		11 pm	3rd " " O 4 b 8.6 40 H.E.	
		11 pm	129 How Bty " O 5 b 1.1½ 10 H.E. 6 Sh.	
			above were fired at request of infantry on points chosen by them at 11 pm (German midnight)	
			Losses during month:-	
	2		Sgt RENNAERT wounded	
	14		[illegible] LEGRAND "	
	16		Lieut COUTELIER "	
	12		Sgt GENON killed	
	16		[illegible] FIEVET wounded	
	18		Gr SIMONIS "	
	22		" AERTS "	
	22		" DELATTE "	
	23		" DESMET "	
	23		" BAELE "	
	24		Lieut SCHIEVELAMP killed	
	27		[illegible] WYNS wounded	
	27		[illegible] DESCHEUVER "	
			Map referred to YPRES. Sheet 28. 1/40000 and 1/10000 Trench sheets of same map.	
			4th Bties of 7th Regiment Belgian Field Artillery H23 b 5 5 attached III Division [illegible] on our left 50th Division. On our right Canadian Division.	

Army Form C. 2118

46

Instructions regarding War Diaries and Intelligence Summaries are contained in F. S. Regs., Part II. and the Staff Manual respectively. Title Pages will be prepared in manuscript.

WAR DIARY
or
INTELLIGENCE SUMMARY

(Erase heading not required.)

Place	Date	Hour	Summary of Events and Information	Remarks and references to Appendices
			War Diary for February 1916. of 7th Regiment Belgian Field Artillery. Vol XII Nail Ward Lieut. RA. Liaison Officer.	

1875 Wt. W593/826 1,000,000 4/15 J.B.C. & A. A.D.S.S./Forms/C. 2118.

Instructions regarding War Diaries and Intelligence Summaries are contained in F. S. Regs., Part II. and the Staff Manual respectively. Title Pages will be prepared in manuscript.

WAR DIARY
or
~~INTELLIGENCE SUMMARY~~
(Erase heading not required.)

Army Form C. 2118

123

Place	Date	Hour	Summary of Events and Information	Remarks and references to Appendices
	1916 Febr 1st	11.10 am	1st Bely. trenches 33-34 Initiative. 40 shr.–	
		2.30	1st Bely completely relieved by the 49th Bty RFA, and moving to the wagon line.	
	2		Whole regiment marched to BOESCHEPE where it remained till Feb. 5th excepting the amm. col. which remained at WESTOUTRE.	
	6		Regiment marched to ARNEKE to billets	
	7		" " " ZUTKERKE to billets	
	8		" " " GUINES where the batteries separated to go to their permanent rest billets as follows– H.Q. of Regiment & 1st Group & 1st & 2nd Btes – WISSANT 3rd Bty & 6th Bty – TARDINGHEN H.Q. 2nd Group – 4th & 5th Btes – AUDINGHEN.	
	17		By order of II Army H.Q. the 1st Group of 3 batteries proceeded to CALAIS and fired trials with French H.E. and Shrapnell (obus à balles) Results were satisfactory.	

1875 Wt. W593/826 1,000,000 4/15 I.B.C. & A. A.D.S.S./Forms/C. 2118.

Instructions regarding War Diaries and Intelligence Summaries are contained in F. S. Regs., Part II. and the Staff Manual respectively. Title Pages will be prepared in manuscript.

WAR DIARY
or
~~INTELLIGENCE SUMMARY~~
(Erase heading not required.)

Army Form C. 2118

124

Place	Date	Hour	Summary of Events and Information	Remarks and references to Appendices
	1916 Feb 25		The 2nd Group of 3 batteries repeated the trial of ammunition and the satisfactory results were confirmed.	
	29		Regiment in rest billets. Casualties nil.	
			Headquarters of unit while in action H23d5.5 map 1/20,000 YPRES. Regt then attached III Division ditto while in rest - WISSANT, mid-way between CALAIS & BOULOGNE, regiment administered by R.A. II Army while in rest.	
			Neil Wood Lieut R.A. Liaison Officer 7th Belgian Field Artillery	

1875 Wt. W593/826 1,000,000 4/15 J.B.C. & A. A.D.S.S./Forms/C. 2118.

Instructions regarding War Diaries and Intelligence Summaries are contained in F. S. Regs., Part II. and the Staff Manual respectively. Title Pages will be prepared in manuscript.

WAR DIARY
or
~~INTELLIGENCE SUMMARY~~
(Erase heading not required.)

Army Form C. 2118

46

Place	Date	Hour	Summary of Events and Information	Remarks and references to Appendices
			War Diary for March 1916 of 7th Belgian Field Artillery, attd V Corps (3rd + 50th Div) B.E.F.	
			Vol XIII	
			Neilwood Lieut. R.A. Liaison Officer.	

1875 Wt. W593/826 1,000,000 4/15 J.B.C. & A. A.D.S.S./Forms/C. 2118.

Instructions regarding War Diaries and Intelligence Summaries are contained in F. S. Regs., Part II. and the Staff Manual respectively. Title Pages will be prepared in manuscript.

WAR DIARY
or
~~INTELLIGENCE SUMMARY~~
(Erase heading not required.)

Army Form C. 2118

123

Place	Date 1916	Hour	Summary of Events and Information	Remarks and references to Appendices
	March 1st		Regiment in rest Billets in & around WISSANT, PAS de CALAIS.	
	9		By order of G.H.Q. the regiment marched to CALAIS & was reviewed, together with the 2nd Brigade of Guards, by the Commander-in-chief.	
	12		By order of 2nd Army H.Q. regiment left rest billets in order to be in V Corps area by 15/3/16. Billeted at ZUTKERKE	
	13		" " HARDIFORT	
	14		" " "	
	15		2nd Group of 4th, 5th & 6th Btys inspected by G.O.C. R.A. 2nd Army & marched to wagon lines at H25 d 9.0, H26 c 6.6, H26 c 1.9 Sheet 28 map YPRES 1/20000.	
	16		1st Group of 1st 2nd & 3rd Btys marched to wagon lines at H21 d 9.4, H21 c 9.4, H21 d 4.5. The 1st Group was attached to 3rd Div under the Command of O.C. 23rd Brigade R.F.A. The 2nd Group was attached to 50th Div under Command of O.C. 4th Northumbrian Bde R.F.A.	

Instructions regarding War Diaries and Intelligence Summaries are contained in F. S. Regs., Part II. and the Staff Manual respectively. Title Pages will be prepared in manuscript.

WAR DIARY
or
~~INTELLIGENCE SUMMARY~~
(Erase heading not required.)

Army Form C. 2118

1226

Place	1916 Date Mch	Hour	Summary of Events and Information	Remarks and references to Appendices
			For the special operations of 24/3/16 & after, at S. ELOI, the 2nd Group was lent to the 3rd Div. & placed under the command of O.C. 23rd Brigade R.F.A.	
			The Bty positions were as follow —	
			1st H 28 a 5.0	
			2nd H 34 b 2.8	
			3rd N 5 a 3.8	
			4th H 29 c 7.7	
			5th I 31 b 1.5	
			6th H 36 b 7.6 (one section only, the other not in action)	
			The O.C. 23rd Brigade R.F.A. allotted them the task of forming a barrage south of the ST. ELOI mound.	
			Number of rounds fired during action 5600.	
			Casualties.	
	18 20		Gunner SABLON. L. wounded March 27. Gr. LENAERTS. E.	WOUNDED
			Adjudant DELAVELEYE. E.R. killed.	
			Brigadier HOUBEN. G. wounded	
			Sergeant DETONGRES. J.N. —	
			Gunner DENAMUR. N.H. —	
			map referred to BELGIUM Sheet 28. 1/40.000.	
			H.Q. of 7th Belgian Field Artillery, 17 RUE DE BOESCHEPE, POPERINGHE.	

1875 Wt. W593/826 1,000,000 4/15 J.B.C. & A. A.D.S.S./Forms/C. 2118.

Neil Wood
Lieut R.A.
Liaison Officer.

Instructions regarding War Diaries and Intelligence Summaries are contained in F. S. Regs., Part II. and the Staff Manual respectively. Title Pages will be prepared in manuscript.

WAR DIARY
or
~~INTELLIGENCE SUMMARY~~
(Erase heading not required.)

Army Form C. 2118

46

Place	Date	Hour	Summary of Events and Information	Remarks and references to Appendices
			War diary of 7th Belgian Field artillery. for April 1916. Vol XIV	

1875 Wt. W593/826 1,000,000 4/15 J.B.C. & A. A.D.S.S./Forms/C. 2118.

Instructions regarding War Diaries and Intelligence Summaries are contained in F. S. Regs., Part II. and the Staff Manual respectively. Title Pages will be prepared in manuscript.

WAR DIARY
or
~~INTELLIGENCE SUMMARY~~
(Erase heading not required.)

Army Form C. 2118

125

Place	1916 Date april	Hour	Summary of Events and Information	Remarks and references to Appendices
	1		Regiment attached 3rd Div. V Corps.	
			Positions as follow — (Covering ST. ELOI.)	
			1st Bty H28 c 8.8	
			2nd " H34 b 9.3	
			3rd " N4 b 2.1	
			4th " H29 c 7.8	
			5th " I31 b 1.5	
			6th " (1 section) H36 b 7.6 – 1 section in reserve in wagon line.	
	6		The six batteries were withdrawn from their positions having fired their last round.	
	7		Regiment passed under the administration of Canadian Corps.	
	12		2nd Group attached to 1st Can. Div. for tactics } R.A.C.C 9/225. 12/4/16.	
			1st " " " 2nd " " "	
	13/14		4th Bty occupies position at H24 c 9½.1 } Covering HILL 60.	
			5th " " " " H24 c 9.9	
			6th " in reserve in wagon line.	
	17		Regiment attached to 1st Can. Div. for administration – from 7th – 17th it having been administered by 2nd Can. Div.	
	20/21		1st Bty occupies position at N4 b 8½.8 } Covering ST. ELOI.	
			2nd " " " " H34 c 6½.3½	
	23/24		3rd " " " " H34 b 1.7	

Instructions regarding War Diaries and Intelligence Summaries are contained in F. S. Regs., Part II. and the Staff Manual respectively. Title Pages will be prepared in manuscript.

WAR DIARY
or
~~INTELLIGENCE SUMMARY~~
(Erase heading not required.)

Army Form C. 2118

126

Place	Date 1916 april.	Hour	Summary of Events and Information	Remarks and references to Appendices
			Casualties.	
	26		Sergeant DE GROOTE. H.B.L. wounded.	
	29		Corporal PALMANS. J. telephonist, wounded.	
			Maps referred to BELGIUM, sheet 28 1/40000	
			H.Q of the 7th Belgian Field artillery 17 RUE DE BOESCHEPE. POPERINGHE.	

Neil Wood
Lieut. R.a.
Liaison Officer
7th Belgian Field Artillery

1875 Wt. W593/826 1,000,000 4/15 J.B.C. & A. A.D.S.S./Forms/C. 2118.

46

Army Form C. 2118

Instructions regarding War Diaries and Intelligence Summaries are contained in F. S. Regs., Part II. and the Staff Manual respectively. Title Pages will be prepared in manuscript.

WAR DIARY
or
~~INTELLIGENCE SUMMARY~~

(Erase heading not required.)

Vol 15

Place	Date	Hour	Summary of Events and Information	Remarks and references to Appendices
			War Diary of 7th Belgian Field Artillery for May 1916.	

1875 Wt. W593/826 1,000,000 4/15 J.B.C. & A. A.D.S.S./Forms/C. 2118.

Instructions regarding War Diaries and Intelligence Summaries are contained in F. S. Regs., Part II. and the Staff Manual respectively. Title Pages will be prepared in manuscript.

WAR DIARY
or
INTELLIGENCE SUMMARY
(Erase heading not required.)

Army Form C. 2118

127

Place	Date 1916	Hour	Summary of Events and Information	Remarks and references to Appendices
	May 1st		Regiment attached for administration to 1st Can. Div. 2nd Group of 3 batteries under tactical Command of 1st Can. Divn. — Group H.Q. at BELGIAN CHATEAU (H23 b 6.6) Battery positions. 4th Batt. H24 c 8.3 Wagon-lines:— H25 d 9.0 (Covering Hill 60.) 5th " H24 c.8.8 H26 c 6.6 6th " In rest at wagon-line H26 c 1.9 2nd Group of 3 batteries under tactical Command of 2nd Can. Div. Group H.Q. H28 a 2.0. Battery positions. 1st Batt N4 b 8½.8 Wagon-lines:— H21 c 9.4 (Covering St ELOI) 2nd " H34 c 6½.3½ (one gun N4 b 1.0½) H21 d 9.4 3rd " H34 b 1.7 H21 d 7.5	
	13		Owing to heavy shelling 1st Group wagon lines were moved to:— 1st Batt: G29 b 7.7 2nd " M6 b 9.7 3rd " M6 c 6.6. Regimental H.Q. 17 RUE DE BOESCHEPE. POPERINGHE. Map referred to BELGIUM. Sheet 28. 1/40000. Owing to bad cartridge cases batteries were ordered by Corps only to fire in case of S.O.S. pending issue of better ammunition.	

Instructions regarding War Diaries and Intelligence Summaries are contained in F. S. Regs., Part II. and the Staff Manual respectively. Title Pages will be prepared in manuscript.

WAR DIARY
or
~~INTELLIGENCE SUMMARY~~
(Erase heading not required.)

Army Form C. 2118

128

Place	Date 1916	Hour	Summary of Events and Information	Remarks and references to Appendices
	May		Casualties during month:—	
	1st		Gr VAN TROYS. C. wounded	
	4		" VERHAEGEN J. A. killed	
	10		" SANCTORUM. A. wounded	
	13		" GUILMIN. J. killed	
	19		" HONGERLOOT. G. E. wounded	
	28		" BUYCK. J. G. "	

Railwood Lieut. R.a.
Liaison Officer
7th Belgian Field Artillery.

1875 Wt. W593/826 1,000,000 4/15 J.B.C. & A. A.D.S.S./Forms/C. 2118.

46

Army Form C. 2118

Instructions regarding War Diaries and Intelligence Summaries are contained in F. S. Regs., Part II. and the Staff Manual respectively. Title Pages will be prepared in manuscript.

WAR DIARY

or

~~INTELLIGENCE SUMMARY~~

(Erase heading not required.)

Vol 16

Place	Date	Hour	Summary of Events and Information	Remarks and references to Appendices
			War Diary for month of June 1916.	
			of	
			7th Belgian Field Artillery attached Canadian Corps.	
			Neil Wood Lieut. R.A. Liaison Officer.	

1875 Wt. W593/826 1,000,000 4/15 J.B.C. & A. A.D.S.S./Forms/C. 2118.

Instructions regarding War Diaries and Intelligence Summaries are contained in F. S. Regs., Part II. and the Staff Manual respectively. Title Pages will be prepared in manuscript.

WAR DIARY
or
~~INTELLIGENCE SUMMARY~~
(Erase heading not required.)

Army Form C. 2118

128

Place	Date	Hour	Summary of Events and Information	Remarks and references to Appendices
	1916 June 1.		Regiment attached for administration to 1st Canadian Division.	
			Positions: 1st Group H.Q. H28 a 2.0. — Wagon lines:–	
			1st Bty N4 b 8½.8 — G29 b 7.7	
			2nd " H34 c 6½.3½ (one gun N4 b 1.0½) — M6 b 9.7.	
			3rd " H34 b 1.7 — M6 c 6.6.	
			Covering St ELOI under direct tactical command of 2nd Can. Div. Arty.	
			2nd Group H.Q. BELGIAN CHATEAU (H23 b 6.6) Wagon-lines:–	
			4th Bty. H24 c 8.3 — H.25 d 9.0	
			5th " H24 c 8.8. — H.26 c. 6.6	
			6th " In rest at Wagon line. — H.26 c. 1.9.	
			Covering HILL 60 and, if necessary, THE BLUFF, under command	of O.C. 5th Bde C.D.A.
	12	4 pm	By order of 2nd Army a trial of ammunition was carried out by 4th Belgian Bty to test cartridge cases. 400 rounds H.E. were fired on HILL 60 and CATERPILLAR, in the presence of Major KELLY, I.O.O. 2nd Army. This Officer reported that the cases were faulty and recommended that a careful inspection should be made for flaws, at the Base. Up to this date the Belgian Batteries had orders only to fire in case of S.O.S., but after this trial the G.O.C.R.A. Canadian Corps, in agreement with Gen: DECHESNE, cdg the 7th Belgian Regt, decided that, if great care were taken in selecting rounds to be fired, the Batteries might be used, as required, by the C.R.A.	
	30		Batteries in same positions.	

1875 Wt. W593/826 1,000,000 4/15 J.B.C. & A. A.D.S.S./Forms/C. 2118.

WAR DIARY
or
~~INTELLIGENCE SUMMARY~~

(Erase heading not required.)

Army Form C. 2118

Instructions regarding War Diaries and Intelligence Summaries are contained in F. S. Regs., Part II. and the Staff Manual respectively. Title Pages will be prepared in manuscript.

129

Place	Date 1916	Hour	Summary of Events and Information	Remarks and references to Appendices
	June		Regimental H.Q. 17 rue de BOESCHEPE, POPERINGHE.	
			Map referred to BELGIUM. Sheet 28. 1/40000.	
			Casualties during month	
	9		Gr. CARPENTIER. O. wounded.	
			Neil Wood Lieut. R.A. Liaison Officer 7th Belgian Field Artillery.	

1875 Wt. W593/826 1,000,000 4/15 J.B.C. & A. A.D.S.S./Forms/C. 2118.

-46

Army Form C. 2118

Instructions regarding War Diaries and Intelligence Summaries are contained in F. S. Regs., Part II. and the Staff Manual respectively. Title Pages will be prepared in manuscript.

WAR DIARY
or
~~INTELLIGENCE SUMMARY~~
(Erase heading not required.)

Vol 17

Place	Date	Hour	Summary of Events and Information	Remarks and references to Appendices
			War Diary of 7th Belgian Field Artillery attached Canadian Corps for July 1916.	
			Rillard Lieut. RA. Liaison Officer.	

1875 Wt. W593/826 1,000,000 4/15 J.B.C. & A. A.D.S.S./Forms/C. 2118.

Instructions regarding War Diaries and Intelligence Summaries are contained in F. S. Regs., Part II. and the Staff Manual respectively. Title Pages will be prepared in manuscript.

WAR DIARY
or
~~INTELLIGENCE SUMMARY~~
(Erase heading not required.)

Army Form C. 2118

130.

Place	Date	Hour	Summary of Events and Information	Remarks and references to Appendices
	1916 July 1		Regiment attached for administration to 1st Canadian Division.	
			Positions:- 1st Group H.Q. H28 a 2.0 — Wagon lines	
			1st Bty N4 b 8½.8 — G29 b 7.7	
			2nd " H34 C 6½.3½ (1 gun N4 b 1.0½) — M6 b 9.7	
			3rd " H34 b 1.7 — M6 C 6.6.	
			Covering St. ELOI under tactical command of O.C. 6th Brigade, 2nd Canadian Div. Arty.	
			Positions:- 2nd Group H.Q. BELGIAN CHATEAU (H23 b 6.6) — Wagon-lines	
			4th Bty H24 C 8.3 — H25 d 9.0	
			5th " In rest at wagon line — H26 C 6.6	
			6th " H24 C 8.8 — H26 C 1.9.	
			Covering Hill 60 and, if necessary, THE BLUFF, under tactical command of O.C. 3rd Brigade 1st Canadian Div. Arty.	
	3~~0~~1		Batteries occupying same positions.	
	14.		Owing to severe bombardment of POPERINGHE, the regimental H.Q. was removed from 17 RUE DE BOESCHEPE, POPERINGHE to the Amm. Col. at M3 C 2.2.	

1875 Wt. W593/826 1,000,000 4/15 J.B.C. & A. A.D.S.S./Forms/C. 2118.

Instructions regarding War Diaries and Intelligence Summaries are contained in F. S. Regs., Part II. and the Staff Manual respectively. Title Pages will be prepared in manuscript.

WAR DIARY
or
~~INTELLIGENCE SUMMARY~~
(Erase heading not required.)

Army Form C. 2118

131

Place	Date 1916	Hour	Summary of Events and Information	Remarks and references to Appendices
	July		Losses during month.	
	9		M.T. Dr PONCELET. E. wounded - died on 11/7/16.	
	12		Sergeant LEMAIRE. L. —"—	
	14		Lieutenant. GRÉGOIRE. A. —"—	
			Gr MASSART. J. —"—	
	29		Gr HAERINCK. H. —"—	
			Gr VERMEULEN. A. —"—	
	30		Sergeant DE BRACKELL. H. —"—	
			Regimental H.Q. M3c2.2.	
			Map referred to Belgium Sheet 28. 1/40000.	

Noël Wood
Lieut. RA.
Liaison Officer.
7th Belgian Field Artillery.

1875 Wt. W593/826 1,000,000 4/15 J.B.C. & A. A.D.S.S./Forms/C. 2118.

D.A.G.
3rd Echelon.

Herewith please find War Diary of this unit for August.

Noël Wood
Lieut. R.A.
Liaison Officer
for H.Q. 7th Belgian Field Artillery

31/8/16.

46

Army Form C. 2118

WAR DIARY

or

~~INTELLIGENCE SUMMARY~~

(Erase heading not required.)

Instructions regarding War Diaries and Intelligence Summaries are contained in F. S. Regs., Part II. and the Staff Manual respectively. Title Pages will be prepared in manuscript.

Vol 18

Place	Date	Hour	Summary of Events and Information	Remarks and references to Appendices
			War Diary for August 1916. of 7th Belgian Field Artillery. [illegible] Lieut RA. Liaison Officer.	

1875 Wt. W593/826 1,000,000 4/15 J.B.C. & A. A.D.S.S./Forms/C. 2118.

Instructions regarding War Diaries and Intelligence Summaries are contained in F. S. Regs., Part II. and the Staff Manual respectively. Title Pages will be prepared in manuscript.

WAR DIARY
or
~~INTELLIGENCE SUMMARY~~
(Erase heading not required.)

Army Form C. 2118

132

Place	Date 1916	Hour	Summary of Events and Information	Remarks and references to Appendices
	Aug.	1.	Regiment attached for administration to 1st Canadian Division.	
			Positions:– 1st Group H.Q. H28a 2.0 — Wagon-lines.	
			1st Bty N4b 8½.8 — C29b 7.7	
			2nd ″ H34c 6½.3½ (1 gun N4b1.0½) — M6b 9.4	
			3rd ″ H34b 1.7 — M6c 6.6	
			Covering St ELOI under tactical command of O.C. 6th Brigade, 2nd Canadian Div. Arty.	
			Positions:– 2nd Group H.Q. BELGIAN CHATEAU (H23b6.6) — Wagon-lines.	
			4th Bty H24c 8.3 — H25d 9.0	
			5th ″ H24c 8.8 — H26c 6.6	
			6th ″ In rest at Wagon-line — H26c 1.9	
			Covering from HILL 60 to THE BLUFF, under tactical command of O.C. 3rd Brigade 1st Canadian Div. Arty.	
		11	2nd Group passed to tactical command of 3rd Canadian Div. Arty. Batteries occupying same positions + covering same zones.	
		14	Regiment passed for administration to 2nd Canadian Division	
		24	″ ″ ″ ″ ″ 4th ″ ″	
		27	2nd Group passed to tactical command of O.C. Right Group, 4th Imperial Division	
			1st Group ″ ″ ″ ″ ″ C.R.A. 4th ANZAC Division	
		31	Units in same positions	

1875 Wt. W593/826 1,000,000 4/15 J.B.C. & A. A.D.S.S./Forms/C. 2118.

Instructions regarding War Diaries and Intelligence Summaries are contained in F. S. Regs., Part II. and the Staff Manual respectively. Title Pages will be prepared in manuscript.

WAR DIARY
or
~~INTELLIGENCE SUMMARY~~

(Erase heading not required.)

Army Form C. 2118

133

Place	Date	Hour	Summary of Events and Information	Remarks and references to Appendices
	1916 Aug.		Casualties during month. Nil.	
			Regimental H.Q. M 3 c 2 2.	
			Map referred to Belgium Sheet 28. 1/40,000.	
			Nailwood [?] Lieut. R.A. Liaison Officer 7th Belgian Field Artillery	

Ba. 4.

D. A. G.
3rd Echelon.

Herewith please find War Diary of this Unit for September.

N. Ellwood
Lieut. R.A.
Liaison Officer
for O.C. 7th Belgian Field Artillery

1/10/16.

Army Form C. 2118 46

WAR DIARY
or
~~INTELLIGENCE SUMMARY~~
(Erase heading not required.)

Instructions regarding War Diaries and Intelligence Summaries are contained in F. S. Regs., Part II. and the Staff Manual respectively. Title Pages will be prepared in manuscript.

Vol 19

Place	Date	Hour	Summary of Events and Information	Remarks and references to Appendices
			War Diary for September 1916 of 7th Belgian Field Artillery.	
			Maillard [?] Lieut. R.A. Liaison Officer.	

1875 Wt. W593/826 1,000,000 4/15 J.B.C. & A. A.D.S.S./Forms/C. 2118.

Instructions regarding War Diaries and Intelligence Summaries are contained in F. S. Regs., Part II. and the Staff Manual respectively. Title Pages will be prepared in manuscript.

WAR DIARY
or
~~INTELLIGENCE SUMMARY~~
(Erase heading not required.)

Army Form C. 2118

134

Place	Date 1916	Hour	Summary of Events and Information	Remarks and references to Appendices
	Sept. 1.		Regiment attached for administration to 4th Canadian Division	
			Positions:— 1st Group H.Q. H28a2.0 — Wagon lines:—	
			1st Bty N4b8½.8 — G29b7.7	
			2nd " H34c6½.8½ (1 gun N4b1.0½) — M6b9.7	
			3rd " H34b1.7 — M6c6.6.	
			Covering St ELOI under tactical command of C.R.A. 4th ANZAC Division (acting as 4th Canadian Div. Arty)	
			Positions:— 2nd Group H.Q. Belgian Château (H23b6.6) — Wagon-lines:—	
			4th Bty H24c8.3 — H25d9.0	
			5th " In rest at wagon-line — H26c6.6	
			6th " H24c8.8 — H26c1.9	
			Covering from HILL 60 to THE BLUFF, under tactical command of O.C. Right Group, 4th Imperial Division	
	10		3rd Bty waggon-line was removed to M6b2.5 from M6c6.6 on account of bad approach to latter position	
	4/5		2nd Group passed to tactical command of O.C. 2nd Brigade, Right Group, 1st ANZAC Division.	
	18		Regiment passed for administration to 1st ANZAC Corps.	
	20		" " " " " 4th ANZAC Division	

Instructions regarding War Diaries and Intelligence Summaries are contained in F. S. Regs., Part II. and the Staff Manual respectively. Title Pages will be prepared in manuscript.

WAR DIARY

or

~~INTELLIGENCE SUMMARY~~

(Erase heading not required.)

Army Form C. 2118

135

Place	Date 1916	Hour	Summary of Events and Information	Remarks and references to Appendices
	Sept.		Casualties during month:—	
			Nil.	
			Regimental H.Q. M 3 c 2.2.	
			Map referred to. Belgium Sheet 28 1/40000.	
			Hailwood Lieut. R.A. Liaison Officer 7th Belgian Field Artillery.	

1875 Wt. W593/826 1,000,000 4/15 J.B.C. & A. A.D.S.S./Forms/C. 2118.

Ba. 8.

D. A. C.
3rd Echelon.

Please find herewith War Diary of this unit for October

Nai Mead
Lieut. R.A.
Liaison Offr. for O.C. 7th Belgian Field Arty.

31/10/16.

46

Instructions regarding War Diaries and Intelligence Summaries are contained in F. S. Regs., Part II. and the Staff Manual respectively. Title pages will be prepared in manuscript.

Army Form C. 2118.

WAR DIARY
or
~~INTELLIGENCE SUMMARY~~. 7 Belgian Fd Art

(Erase heading not required.)

Vol 20

Place	Date	Hour	Summary of Events and Information	Remarks and references to Appendices
			War Diary for October 1916 of 7th Belgian Field Artillery.	
			Railtherd Lieut. R.A. Liaison Officer.	

2353 Wt. W2544/1454 700,000 5/15 D. D. & L. A.D.S.S./Forms/C. 2118.

Instructions regarding War Diaries and Intelligence Summaries are contained in F. S. Regs., Part II. and the Staff Manual respectively. Title pages will be prepared in manuscript.

WAR DIARY
or
~~INTELLIGENCE SUMMARY.~~
(Erase heading not required.)

Army Form C. 2118.

136.

Place	Date 1916	Hour	Summary of Events and Information	Remarks and references to Appendices
	Oct.			
	1.		Regiment attached for administration to 4th Australian Division.	
			Positions:— 1st Group H.Q. H28 a 2.0 — Wagon lines:—	
			1st Bty N4 b 8½.8 — C29 b 7.7	
			2nd " H34 c 6½.8½ (1 gun N4 b 1.0½) — M6 b 9.7	
			3rd " H34 b 1.7 — M6 b 2.5	
			Covering 51. E.L.01 under tactical command of C.R.A. 4th Australian Divn	
			Positions:— 2nd Group H.Q. Belgian Chateau (H23 b 6.6) — Wagon lines.	
			4th Bty H24 c 8.3 — H25 d 9.0	
			5th " In rest at wagon line — H26 c 6.6	
			6th H24 c 8.8 — H26 c 1.9	
			Covering from HILL 60 to THE BLUFF under tactical command of O.C. Right Group, 1st Australian Divn	
	15		2nd Group passed to command of 4th Australian Divn (O.C. 11th Bde A.F.A.)	
			5th Bty went into position at I19 a 2.7, relieving 102nd Bty 1st Aus. Div. Arty.	
			On account of the extension of 4th Aus. Divn the Belgian Groups altered	

2353 Wt. W2544/1454 700,000 5/15 D. D. & L. A.D.S.S./Forms/C. 2118.

Instructions regarding War Diaries and Intelligence Summaries are contained in F. S. Regs., Part II. and the Staff Manual respectively. Title pages will be prepared in manuscript.

WAR DIARY
or
INTELLIGENCE SUMMARY.
(Erase heading not required.)

Army Form C. 2118.

137.

Place	Date	Hour	Summary of Events and Information	Remarks and references to Appendices
	1916 Oct			
	15		Gun emplacements so as to cover following zones:—	
			1st Group, from RUINED FARM (O3c 8.4) to VIERSTRAAT ROAD (N18b 2.5)	
			2nd " from RUINED FARM to HILL 60	
	22		2nd Group passed to tactical command of 47th Divn (O.C. 235th Bde R.F.A.)	
	24		Regiment passed for administration to 41st Divn. 1st Group remaining tactically under command of C.R.A. 4th Aus. Divn, which was acting as 41st Div. Arty.	
	22		5th Bty was relieved at I19a 2.7 by How. Bty of 47th Div. Arty, and took up position at I19a 4.6.	
	31		Same positions	
			Casualties during October	
	12		Gr MEYNEN. H. Wounded	
	22		Sgt BRASSEUR. R. "	
	22		Gr BOUILLON. E. "	
	23		Gr DE WAEGENEER. D. Killed	
			Regimental H.Q. M 3c 2.2. Map referred to Belgium Sheet 28. 1/40000.	

Vaillant(?) Lieut. Ra.
Liaison Officer.
7th Belgian Field artillery

2353 Wt. W2544/1454 700,000 5/15 D. D. & L. A.D.S.S./Forms/C. 2118.

B.a. 10

D.A.G.
3rd Echelon

Please find herewith War Diary of this Unit for November 1916. Also Duplicate Copies for June, July, August and September 1916.

Noël Wood
Lieut. R.A.
Liaison Officer
for O.C. 7th Belgian Field Artillery

30/11/16.

Instructions regarding War Diaries and Intelligence Summaries are contained in F. S. Regs., Part II. and the Staff Manual respectively. Title pages will be prepared in manuscript.

WAR DIARY
or
~~INTELLIGENCE SUMMARY.~~
(*Erase heading not required.*)

Army Form C. 2118. 46

Vol 21

Place	Date	Hour	Summary of Events and Information	Remarks and references to Appendices
			War Diary of 7th Belgian Field Artillery for November 1916.	
			Noël Wood Lieut. RA Liaison Officer.	

2353 Wt. W2544/1454 700,000 5/15 D. D. & L. A.D.S.S./Forms/C. 2118.

Instructions regarding War Diaries and Intelligence Summaries are contained in F. S. Regs., Part II. and the Staff Manual respectively. Title pages will be prepared in manuscript.

WAR DIARY
or
~~INTELLIGENCE SUMMARY.~~
(Erase heading not required.)

Army Form C. 2118.

138.

Place	Date	Hour	Summary of Events and Information	Remarks and references to Appendices
	1916 Nov. 1.		Regiment attached for administration to 41st Division.	
			Positions:– 1st Group H.Q. H28a2·0 — Wagon-lines:–	
			1st Bty N4b8½·8 — C29b7·7	
			2nd " H34c5·3 (1 emplacement N4b1·0½) — M6b9·7	
			3rd " H34b1·7 — M6b2·5	
			Covering from VIERSTRAAT Rd (N18b2·5) to RUINED FARM (O3c8·4), under tactical command of C.R.A. 4th Australian Division (acting 41st Div. Arty.)	
			Positions:– 2nd Group. H.Q. Belgian Château (H23b6·6) — Wagon-lines:–	
			4th Bty H24c8·3 — H25d9·0	
			5th " (one section) I19a4·6 — H26c6·6	
			6th " H24c8·8 — H26c1·9	
			Covering from RUINED FARM (O3c8·4) to H12b0, under tactical command of 47th Division (O.C. 235th Bde R.F.A.)	
	14		1st Group passed to tactical command of C.R.A. 41st Div. Arty.	
	20		5th Bty moved its section from I19a4·6 to new emplacements at H24b6·3.	
	30		Units in same positions.	

Instructions regarding War Diaries and Intelligence Summaries are contained in F. S. Regs., Part II. and the Staff Manual respectively. Title pages will be prepared in manuscript.

WAR DIARY
or
INTELLIGENCE SUMMARY.
(Erase heading not required.)

Army Form C. 2118.

139.

Place	Date 1916	Hour	Summary of Events and Information	Remarks and references to Appendices
	Nov.		Casualties during November: —	
	"	1.	Gr. OUDENARDE. F. wounded.	
			Regimental H.Q. M3C2.2.	
			Map referred to Belgium Sheet 28 1/40,000.	
			Noël Wood Lieut. R.A. Liaison Officer 7th Belgian Field Artillery	

2353 Wt. W2544/1454 700,000 5/15 D. D. & L. A.D.S.S./Forms/C. 2118.

Ba. 11.

D.A.G.
3rd Echelon

Please find herewith the War Diary of this Unit for December 1916.

Naïlwood
Lieut. R.A.
Liaison Officer
13th (old 7th) Belgian Field Artillery

31/12/16.

Instructions regarding War Diaries and Intelligence Summaries are contained in F. S. Regs., Part II. and the Staff Manual respectively. Title pages will be prepared in manuscript.

WAR DIARY
or
~~INTELLIGENCE SUMMARY~~.
(Erase heading not required.)

Army Form C. 2118.

46

Vol 22

Place	Date	Hour	Summary of Events and Information	Remarks and references to Appendices
			War Diary for December 1916 of 13th (old 7th) Belgian Field Artillery.	
			Hailwood Lieut. RA. Liaison Officer.	

2353 Wt. W2514/1454 700,000 5/15 D. D. & L. A.D.S.S./Forms/C. 2118.

Instructions regarding War Diaries and Intelligence Summaries are contained in F. S. Regs., Part II. and the Staff Manual respectively. Title pages will be prepared in manuscript.

WAR DIARY
or
~~INTELLIGENCE SUMMARY.~~
(*Erase heading not required.*)

Army Form C. 2118.

140.

Place	Date	Hour	Summary of Events and Information	Remarks and references to Appendices
	1916 Dec. 1		Regiment attached for administration to 41st Division.	
			Positions:— 1st Group H.Q. H28a2.0 — Wagon-lines:—	—
			1st Bty N4b8½.8 — G29b7.7	
			2nd " H34c5.3 (1 emplacement N4b1.0½) — M6b9.7	
			3rd " H34b1.7 — M6b2.5	
			Covering from VIERSTRAAT Rd (N18b2.5) to RUINED FARM (O3c8.4) under tactical command of C.R.A. 41st Division.	
			Positions:— 2nd Group H.Q. Belgian Château (H23b6.6) — Wagon-lines:—	
			4th Bty H24c8.3 — H25d9.0	
			5th " (one section) H24b6.3 — H26c6.6	
			6th " H24c8.8 — H26c1.9	
			Covering from RUINED FARM (O3c8.4) to Hill 60. under tactical command of 47th Division	
	10 30		Owing to re-organisation of Belgian army, the number of the regiment is changed from 7 to 13. Units in same positions.	
			Casualties: Wounded:— Adjudant FIEVET. P.F., Sgt GARA. A.G., Gr DESUTTER. C.G.	
			Regimental H.Q. M3c2.2. Map referred to Belgium Sheet 28 1/40,000.	

Noël Wood
Lieut. R.A.
Liaison Officer
13th (old 7th) Belgian Field Artillery

www.ingramcontent.com/pod-product-compliance
Lightning Source LLC
Chambersburg PA
CBHW081541160426
43191CB00011B/1809
* 9 7 8 1 4 7 4 5 2 1 2 1 5 *